33,260

P9-DCI-675

THE WAY
PEOPLE
LIVE

Life in the South During the Civil War

Titles in The Way People Live series include:

Cowboys in the Old West
Life During the French Revolution
Life in Ancient Greece
Life in Ancient Rome
Life in an Eskimo Village
Life in the Elizabethan Theater
Life in the North During the Civil War
Life in the South During the Civil War
Life in the Warsaw Ghetto
Life in War-Torn Bosnia
Life on a Medieval Pilgrimage
Life on an Israeli Kibbutz

THE WAY
PEOPLE
LIVE

Life in the South During the Civil War

by James P. Reger

Lucent Books, P.O. Box 289011, San Diego, CA 92198-9011

Library of Congress Cataloging-in-Publication Data

Reger, James P.
    Life in the South during the Civil War / by James P. Reger.
        p.   cm. — (The way people live)
    Includes bibliographical references and index.
    Summary: Describes the daily life, in the Confederacy, of ladies and
gentlemen, slaves, middle-class whites, and marginal characters.
    ISBN 1-56006-333-5 (alk. paper)
    1. Confederate States of America—Social life and customs—Juvenile
literature.   [1. Confederate States of America—Social life and customs.]
I. Title.   II. Series.
E487.R34   1997
975'.03—dc20   96-26353
                                                                                      CIP
                                                                                      AC

Copyright 1997 by Lucent Books, Inc., P.O. Box 289011, San Diego, California,
92198-9011

Printed in the U.S.A.

Contents

Discovering the Humanity in Us All

The Way People Live series focuses on pockets of human culture. Some of these are current cultures, like the Eskimos of the Arctic; others no longer exist, such as the Jewish ghetto in Warsaw during World War II. What many of these cultural pockets share, however, is the fact that they have been viewed before, but not completely understood.

To really understand any culture, it is necessary to strip the mind of the common notions we hold about groups of people. These stereotypes are the archenemies of learning. It does not even matter whether the stereotypes are positive or negative; they are confining and tight. Removing them is a challenge that's not easily met, as anyone who has ever tried it will admit. Ideas that do not fit into the templates we create are unwelcome visitors—ones we would prefer remain quietly in a corner or forgotten room.

The cowboy of the Old West is a good example of such confining roles. The cowboy was courageous, yet soft-spoken. His time (it is always a he, in our template) was spent alternatively saving a rancher's daughter from certain death on a runaway stagecoach, or shooting it out with rustlers. At times, of course, he was likely to get a little crazy in town after a trail drive, but for the most part, he was the epitome of inner strength. It is disconcerting to find out that the cowboy is human, even a bit childish. Can it really be true that cowboys would line up to help the cook on the trail drive grind coffee, just hoping he would give them a little stick of pep-

permint candy that came with the coffee shipment? The idea of tough cowboys vying with one another to help "Coosie" (as they called their cooks) for a bit of candy seems silly and out of place.

So is the vision of Eskimos playing video games and watching MTV, living in prefab housing in the Arctic. It just does not fit with what "Eskimo" means. We are far more comfortable with snow igloos and whale blubber, harpoons and kayaks.

Although the cultures dealt with in Lucent's The Way People Live series are often historically and socially well known, the emphasis is on the personal aspects of life. Groups of people, while unquestionably affected by their politics and their governmental structures, are more than those institutions. How do people in a particular time and place educate their children? What do they eat? And how do they build their houses? What kinds of work do they do? What kinds of games do they enjoy? The answers to these questions bring these cultures to life. People's lives are revealed in the particulars and only by knowing the particulars can we understand these cultures' will to survive and their moments of weakness and greatness.

This is not to say that understanding politics does not help to understand a culture. There is no question that the Warsaw ghetto, for example, was a culture that was brought about by the politics and social ideas of Adolf Hitler and the Third Reich. But the Jews who were crowded together in the ghetto cannot be understood by the Reich's politics. Their life was a day-to-day battle for existence, and the creativity and methods they used to prolong their lives is a vital story of human perseverance that would be denied by focusing only on the institutions of Hitler's Germany. Knowing that children as young as five or six outwitted Nazi guards on a daily basis, that Jewish policemen helped the Germans control the ghetto, that children attended secret schools in the ghetto and even earned diplomas—these are the things that reveal the fabric of life, that can inspire, intrigue, and amaze.

Books in the The Way People Live series allow both the casual reader and the student to see humans as victims, heroes, and onlookers. And although humans act in ways that can fill us with feelings of sorrow and revulsion, it is important to remember that "hero," "predator," and "victim" are dangerous terms. Heaping undue pity or praise on people reduces them to objects, and strips them of their humanity.

Seeing the Jews of Warsaw only as victims is to deny their humanity. Seeing them only as they appear in surviving photos, staring at the camera with infinite sadness, is limiting, both to them and to those who want to understand them. To an object of pity, the only appropriate response becomes "Those poor creatures!" and that reduces both the quality of their struggle and the depth of their despair. No one is served by such two-dimensional views of people and their cultures.

With this in mind, the The Way People Live series strives to flesh out the traditional, two-dimensional views of people in various cultures and historical circumstances. Using a wide variety of primary quotations—the words not only of the politicians and government leaders, but of the real people whose lives are being examined—each book in the series attempts to show an honest and complete picture of a culture removed from our own by time or space.

By examining cultures in this way, the reader will notice not only the glaring differences from his or her own culture, but also will be struck by the similarities. For indeed, people share common needs—warmth, good company, stability, and affirmation from others. Ultimately, seeing how people really live, or have lived can only enrich our understanding of ourselves.

The Homecoming

Everything smelled burnt and sooty to the defeated Confederate soldiers returning home from the Civil War. The woods, the sky, the fields, and the towns all reeked with a nose-twinging bitterness bordering on the sour. In many places a brown haze still hung over the smoldering ruins of houses, barns, and other civilian enclaves; a smog that possessed a strangely reminiscent putridity. It was the sulphurous stench of dead and dying flesh, and it nauseated even these hardened battle survivors to smell it here.

They had almost gotten accustomed to the stench of half-buried bodies near field hospitals and battlefields; that sticky, yellow smell seemed to belong to such places. But it did not belong here—not at home. Not on farms and in towns and civilian refugee camps. Hadn't these men left an earth-

A Confederate soldier (center) stands amidst the ruins of Richmond, Virginia. As the defeated Rebels returned to the South, they found their once magnificent cities and homes obliterated by the war.

Near the close of the war, many Confederate soldiers decided to get a head start on the long journey home. They took to the roads with Union cavalrymen pursuing them in hopes of making them the last prisoners of war. The scrawny Rebels ducked into barns and chicken coops as much to find food as to hide from their potential captors. They sometimes found freedom but they rarely, if ever, found food. The following account is taken from Shelby Foote's The Civil War: A Narrative.

"One bare-footed, filthy skeleton of a Confederate met just that fate near Appomattox Court House, Virginia. Chased down and surrounded by mounted Yankees, he held up his hands to surrender.

'We've got you now,' shouted a well-fed Yankee. He and the other cavalrymen drew their pistols to contain this 'dangerous' man.

But the foul-smelling Rebel gave up without a fight. Collapsing to the ground in fatigue, he replied weakly, 'Yep, you got me, all right. And a hell of a git you got.'"

fragrant and blossoming South? What could have happened to make it stink so sickeningly of rot and death?

Food and Answers

Living hand-to-mouth on the long roads home, the scarecrow veterans took food, comfort, and answers from the few citizens who still had any to give. Their ragged condition shocked the home folk just as much as the condition of the home folk shocked them. One hosting farmer noted:

> They were without homes, had no food, and were in need of clothes and shoes. Many still wore threadbare Confederate uniforms (banned by the Union occupation army) because they had nothing else.[1]

While ravenously devouring whatever morsels they were offered, the soldiers heard tales of marauding Yankees who had devastated the landscape and punished the civilians for the "sins" of the Confederate army.

A Southern woman serves dinner to a hungry Civil War veteran. While enjoying the hospitality of generous Southerners, the returning Rebels were astounded by their hosts' tales of hardship.

Railroads had been ripped up, they were told. Crops and fields had been laid waste. Whatever the Federals had not been able to consume or send to the North, they had simply looted and destroyed. The resulting blight had caused Union general William Sherman, the author of a great portion of the destruction, to remark that "a crow would have to carry its own provender"[2] when it flew over this plundered land.

They heard that some areas were harder hit than others. South Carolina had taken a particularly harsh beating because the Federals held the people there responsible for starting the war. A Connecticut writer who had already seen devastated Columbia, South Carolina, wrote:

The entire heart of the city was a wilderness of crumbling walls, naked chimneys and trees killed by flames. The fountains of the desolated gardens were dry, the basins cracked; the pillars of the houses were dismantled or overthrown; the marble steps were broken. The churches had been pillaged and burned.[3]

On the coast, Charleston escaped total destruction but, according to one Federal officer,

There was no wall and no roof that did not bear eloquent marks of having been under the fire of siege guns. The burned district was one vast grave yard of broken walls and tall blackened chimneys for monuments, overtopped by the picturesque ruins of the Cathedral.[4]

The returning veterans found that even where physical damage was not total, cultural damage was. This was also reflected by a Maine ship's carpenter arriving in nearby Savannah, Georgia. He was shocked to find the once bustling port a deserted, if intact, city. He wrote:

Everything looked very desolate. Nearly all the prominent citizens had abandoned their homes and only the Negroes and whites too poor in purse to get away remained. The wharves, piers, and bulkheads were going to decay and grass and weeds were growing over them. It was indeed sorrowful to know of the sufferings of the Southerner at the close of the war.[5]

Homeless . . . Nationless

The returning rebels felt the same way especially when they encountered the thousands upon thousands of homeless refugees— Southern citizens whom they had sworn themselves to protect—crowding roads that led to nowhere, in search of food, water, shelter, and hope that did not exist. One Confederate wrote of the scene:

Vehicles carry black and white refugees. Such wagons and such horses were surely never seen. Each rivaled the other in protuberance, shakiness, and general disposition to tumble down and dissolve. They all bring saddening stories of destitution.[6]

A Union officer in Atlanta, Georgia, agreed with that Southern veteran when he pointed out that the civilians streaming into the ruined city (some fifty thousand) had little or nothing to eat. He reported:

Women and children walk from ten to forty miles for food and then obtain only a morsel, frequently not any. Intense suffering will follow. Until the crops of this

Since most males between the ages of sixteen and forty-five were still trying to make their way back home from the war, the throngs of civilian refugees crowding the roads were comprised mostly of boys, old men, and women. One young woman who was burned out of her house and forced to survive as a homeless person was Eliza Frances Andrews. She had been educated more thoroughly than most middle-class girls and, as a result, was able to keep an accurate and highly literate diary of her wartime trials. Writing in her War-Time Diary of a Georgia Girl, *she recorded the following observation.*

"About three miles from Sparta, we struck 'burnt country.' The fields were trampled down and the road was lined with carcasses of hogs, horses, and cattle that the invader had wantonly shot down. The stench in some places was unbearable. The dwellings that were standing all showed signs of pillage, and on every plantation we saw the charred remains of the ginhouse. Total homes laid in ashes. Hayricks and fodder stacks were demolished, corn cribs were empty, and every bale of cotton burnt. I saw no grain of any sort except little patches they had spilled when feeding their horses, and there was not even a chicken left in the country to eat. A bag of oats might have lain anywhere along the road without danger from the beasts of the field though I cannot say it would have been safe from the assaults of hungry men."

country are cultivated to maturity, the people here, both black and white, will suffer for food.[7]

And from the richest to the poorest, the blackest to the whitest, that is exactly what they did.

Divergent People/Convergent Hardships

What had happened? these limping, fatigued warriors had to have asked. How could their homes and world have ever disintegrated into this? The returning men represented every class and race of Southerner, and yet none among them could find anything even remotely resembling the lifestyle or civilization they had left.

A Rebel soldier grasps his rifle as he poses for a photograph. The Confederate army comprised men of every race and class, ranging from poor farmers to wealthy planters.

A wounded Rebel soldier finds comfort in the arms of his family. Most soldiers were not so fortunate and returned to families and homes devastated by four destructive years of war.

Blacks who had served their Confederate masters or worked in Southern labor details came home to plantations and farms that were deserted or razed to the ground. Their niches in the social hierarchy, however low, had vanished along with any sense of security and place they might have offered.

The poor whites, who had little more to lose than the blacks, made their way back to their hardscrabble farms with dreams no more ambitious than to resume hunting and fishing and coaxing a few subsistence crops out of the rocky earth. Since they had never owned slaves, they found none missing, but they sometimes discovered newly freed blacks living nearby and competing for the same meager resources.

The middle-class Southerners, a few of whom had spent their life savings to own a slave or two, usually discovered that they were long gone. Their modest farms were often burned or picked clean, their horses and cattle "appropriated." Their homes, solidly built yet unpretentious, still stood if they had been used as a headquarters or if battle had mercifully passed them by.

Otherwise, they most likely had provided tempting targets for pillaging soldiers, who, at the very least, stripped them of everything not nailed down.

But it was the planters, the upper-class leaders of the South, who had gambled the most on victory and, in turn, had lost the most in defeat. As officers, they had proudly ridden off to war on prancing chargers with visions of triumphant homecomings titillating their minds. Those few who had returned, though, were often in rags and on foot. No bands or parades greeted them. And as they walked up the long driveways to where their lavish homes had been, the last vestige of their hopes usually came tumbling down.

Gone was the splendor, the grace, and the elegance in which they and their families had lived. Gone were the mansions, the gardens, and the servants. Perhaps by recalling the last, sweet day of peace, they would have a place to start their search for an understanding of what had gone wrong. At the very least, they might be able to close their eyes and remember the scented blossoms of a spring day four long, long years before.

The Manor, the Man, and the Moment

April 12, 1861, the day the Civil War began with the Confederates attacking Fort Sumter, dawned sunny and blue-skyed across the South. Around the mansions and outbuildings of the enormous plantations, pigs snorted, roosters squawked, and overseers shouted to awaken the slaves in their cabins. The smell of hog fat frying in cast-iron skillets mingled with the wafting, magnolia-scented breeze and paddle wheelers blasted their hoarse steam whistles from the rivers.

To people in the North and the South, scenes such as these evoked a feeling of nostalgia and longing. Plantation life and the plantation character had long possessed a mythical air. One Northern houseguest arising to the typical morning ritual mused:

I cannot help but find myself enamored by the hot land and the crops, the great manor house and outbuildings, the gardens and the river-bordered lawn, grazing animals and playing children, and the Negroes wearing bright-colored cottons and speaking in soft, liquid voices.[8]

The Same Rhythms on a Very Different Day

On this Friday like any other Friday, the timeless rhythms of work continued. That meant that all men, women, and children, black or white, free or slave, would soon be beginning the mandatory tasks assigned to them by their particular planter and would

An idealized painting of a Southern home bustles with horse-drawn carriages as a paddle wheeler makes its way down the nearby Mississippi River.

The Manor, the Man, and the Moment   13

continue those tasks without letup until well after dark. They took comfort, though, in the fact that only one and a half working days were left before the Saturday night dances and the usual day off on Sunday. Little did they know just how much discomfort the events of those fateful days would eventually cause them or how thoroughly they would disrupt the only lifestyle any of them had ever known.

Mary Boykin Chesnut, plantation mistress and wife of a Confederate officer and politician, witnessed those events and recorded their effects in what would become one of the most famous diaries of the era. At 4:00 A.M. Friday morning, April 12, 1861, she jolted awake in her hotel room in Charleston, South Carolina, to the blasts of booming artillery. She immediately jumped out of bed and fell to her knees in prayer.

She later wrote:

I prayed as I had never prayed before. There was a sound of stir all over the house, pattering of feet in the corridors. All seemed hurrying one way. I put on my double gown and a shawl and went too. It was to the housetop. The shells were bursting . . . the regular roar of the cannon! The women were wild there on the housetops. Prayers came from them, and imprecations from the men, and then a shell would light up the scene.[9]

After thirty-six nerve-jangling hours of siege and sleeplessness, the news for which Mrs. Chesnut had been hoping was announced, and it instantly revived her spirits. She wrote:

I did not know that one could live such days of excitement. Fort Sumter has surrendered! It is the liveliest crowd I think I ever saw. Everybody talking at once. This is a grand frolic! The (army) camps are in a fit of horseplay![10]

The Rush to Glory

In the weeks following the Confederate victory at Fort Sumter, this carnival atmosphere

For the many slaves who toiled in the cotton fields of Southern plantations, life was consumed by hard physical labor.

Confederates lay siege to Fort Sumter, the Union garrison in South Carolina. The fall of Fort Sumter inspired many patriotic Rebels to leave the comfort of their homes and join the Confederate army.

spread throughout the rest of the South like a contagion of manic laughter. English journalist William Russell observed "flushed faces, wild eyes, screaming mouths hurrahing for 'Jeff Davis' and the 'Southern Confederacy' so that the yells overpowered the discordant bands which were busy with 'Dixie's Land.'"[11]

At whistle-stops on his troop train, Sam Watkins, a volunteer from Tennessee, saw hundreds of

> Southern cockades [floral ornaments worn as badges] made by ladies and sweethearts, flags made by ladies presented to companies, and young orators telling how they would protect those flags or not come back at all. Citizens were waving their handkerchiefs and hurrahing.[12]

A wealthy planter's son from New Orleans wrote of his send-off:

That certainly was the only time that I can remember when citizens walked along the lines offering their pocketbooks to men whom they did not know; that fair women bestowed their floral offerings and kisses ungrudgingly and with equal favor among all classes of friends and suitors; when the distinctions of society, wealth, and station were forgotten, and each departing soldier was equally honored as a hero.[13]

Mary Chesnut noted in her diary, "Charleston is crowded with soldiers. These new ones are running in, fairly. They fear the war will be over before they get a sight of the fun. Every man from every little country precinct wants a piece of the picture."[14]

Most of them would get that piece, too, in all its lurid color, as would those who

A planter and his wife tour the lush grounds of their Southern plantation. The expansive plantation owners of the South made their fortunes in agriculture, growing such cash crops as cotton, tobacco, and sugarcane.

remained on the home front when the Yankees invaded in earnest. That would not happen for some time, though. Until then, the home life of the Southern people in general and the planter aristocracy in particular would change very little from the way it had thrived for over two hundred years. After all, business was still business. And the business of plantations was agriculture.

A Manor unto Itself

Southern plantation agriculture required the labor of large gangs of black slaves to grow one or two cash crops as well as smaller amounts of traditional edible crops. The planters would take the money earned from selling their cash crops (cotton, tobacco, sugarcane, rice, hemp, or indigo) and buy the manufactured goods that they did not produce themselves. In that way, they acquired the factory-made items they needed to maintain their opulent lifestyles and bought more land and slaves to renew the cycle.

The large plantations could, thus, function as self-contained manors, consisting of the manor house complex, slave quarters for fifty to two hundred slaves, a commissary store, gristmill, warehouse, sawmill, timber operation, cattle herd, barn, butchery, cotton gin, dock, stables, and dozens of workplaces for craftsmen and semiskilled laborers (laundresses, cooks, house servants, and so on). The surrounding land, the plantation's reason for being, could easily take up two thousand acres of the flattest, most fertile land in the South.

Such an estate might stretch for five miles or more from one side to the other and from top to bottom. That meant a person could walk five miles to the north, five miles to the east, five miles to the south, and five miles to the west without ever leaving the property. Incredibly, a few plantations boasted some ten thousand acres, occupying a square twenty-five miles long and twenty-five miles wide.

Texas senator Louis T. Wigfall, an ardent believer in these vast operations, justified them this way:

> We are an agricultural people; we are a primitive but a civilized people. We have no cities. We don't want them! We have

no commercial navy, no military navy. We don't want them! We want no manufactures. We desire no trading, no mechanical, or manufacturing classes. As long as we have our rice, our sugar, our tobacco, and our cotton, we can command the wealth to purchase all we want from those nations with which we are in amity, and to lay up money besides![15]

For the Good of All—Almost

Senator Wigfall may have been overly enthusiastic about the plantation system, but it did, in fact, generate profits, and nearly every businessman who took part in it benefited from its cycle. The planters made money selling their raw cotton, the English made money selling their processed cotton cloth, and the European and New England factory owners made money selling their manufactured goods to the Southerners. The Southerners, in turn, grew more cotton in their expanding fields and started the whole process over again. This arrangement had the added dividend of profiting the brokers, salesmen, bankers, and shippers involved, prompting one Northern merchant to say simply, "Cotton has enriched all through whose hands it has passed." [16]

Remarkably, for all the wealth these grand farm owners generated, they only represented about three thousand family estates throughout the entire South. This reveals some astounding statistics: only about 1 percent of the population owned 25 percent of the slaves, who worked 50 percent of the Southern fields, which grew 50 percent of America's tobacco, 75 percent of its cotton, and 100 percent of its sugar, rice, hemp, and indigo.

It is little wonder that the men who wielded this economic power were often called upon to act as government leaders, political representatives, judges, bankers, and militia commanders, as well as society patrons, pillars of culture, and hosts of the most magnificent socials in the land. It is even less wonder that they took on the name "the planter aristocracy" and considered themselves heirs to the English feudal tradition of knights, damsels, lords, and ladies.

Black slaves return home from the fields with baskets overflowing with cotton. Planters grew rich as their slaves worked in the cotton fields, planting, harvesting, and maintaining the valuable crop.

The Lord's Simple Needs

Each planter envisioned himself as a sovereign ruler reigning justly, wisely, paternally, and firmly over all his "children" (whom he considered incapable of getting along without his guidance and discipline). The planter defined "children" broadly: it included not only the little ones whom he had fathered by his wife, but also his wife, any younger brothers or sisters living with him, the overseers, the employees, the house servants, the craftsmen, the slave drivers, the field hands, and all their offspring.

In return for this paternalistic care, he demanded only two things: honor and absolute obedience. Once satisfied that these had been delivered, the master endeavored to fulfill every physical, emotional, social, and spiritual need that he determined all those beneath him required. When unsatisfied, that master would exact swift and severe retribution from the offending parties whether they be his wife, children, employees, or slaves.

Simply put, the planter was a lord who answered to no one but himself. He had no peers or rivals within the boundaries of his estate, no challengers to his authority. His will, once revealed, became the will of every "subject" under him. If he chose to reign benevolently, his subjects could live in rela-

They Grew What?!

If Southern planters were alive today and growing their usual crops, many would be arrested and sent to jail or at least scorned by the public for adding to the corruption of our youth. Their faces would appear on post office walls, and their stories would be televised on nationwide crime search programs. For they would be guilty of producing a controlled substance, an illegal drug, and in quantities large enough to make millions.

The crop was called hemp, and it produced fibers that grew inside the plant. It was those fibers that the planters sought to harvest and wind into ropes or bundle into bales for sale to other rope makers.

Hemp was a relatively easy, nonlabor-intensive crop for planters to grow. In the spring, their field hands simply scattered the seeds on top of the damp, loamy Southern soil and tamped them gently into ground. Seedlings popped up shortly thereafter and, with rain and proper drainage, they thrived in the mild, moist climate. By the end of the summer, the hemp stalks reached heights of ten to twelve feet, creating a veritable forest beneath which men could become lost.

When the greenish-yellow pollen flowers of the female plants blossomed in the fall, the slaves hacked the towering plants down with machete knives and stripped the extraneous vegetation from them until only the stalks remained. They then hung the viney stems up by the roots to let their tough exteriors rot away. Once sufficiently rotten, the slaves would pull out the interior fibers, dry them, and either bale them or twist them into cordage.

For reasons that many planters never fully understood, they never had trouble getting the blacks to work in the hemp fields, especially at harvesttime. In fact, they often had to turn away workers when too many volunteered for the duty. That was due to the fact that another name for hemp was marijuana, the leaves and buds of which had been a preferred "medicine" of the slaves since their days in the Caribbean.

Slaves pose for a photograph in front of their meager cabin. Although many planters treated their slaves with kindness, stories abound about the cruelty slaves experienced at the hands of their masters.

tive comfort. If, however, he chose to abuse his power, they would undoubtedly suffer.

One South Carolina planter, representing many others, believed that plantation efficiency would be best achieved by treating his slaves gently. He wrote:

> If all men were enjoined to love one another and to contribute as much as possible to the happiness of others, how much more is it the duty of men who hold such command over others as we do our slaves and our families. It is then indisputably our most imperious duty to treat and govern them with a view to their comfort and happiness, as it is consistent with propriety, and the performance of their duties toward us.[17]

Clearly, not all masters felt that way. Robert McAlpin, a transplanted New Englander, developed a huge plantation in Louisiana. He treated his wife, children, and slaves with complete equality: he horribly abused them all.

One witness reported that he "was the cruelest slave owner ever known. So much so that his slaves would sometimes despair and kill themselves." Another said, "He was the worst man in the whole country. He sewed up a nigger in a sack and drowned him in the river."[18]

A third added:

> When he was drunk he would abuse his slaves dreadfully and caused the death of several of them. Once his cook didn't cook dinner to suit him and he whipped her unmercifully, and tied her, entirely naked, to a stake. Then he broke her jaw with his walking stick. She died that night about 9:00 o'clock.[19]

Fortunately, there were more benevolent than cruel slaveholders in the South. In a book entitled *Black Slave Narratives*, the firsthand accounts of the slaves themselves indicate that 70 percent of them were not corporally punished at the hands of their masters, slave drivers, or overseers. Of course, that leaves the other 30 percent, some one million people, who did suffer the physical expression of their masters' wrath.

It is significant to note that while Robert McAlpin was reviled by all the other planters who knew him, he was never prosecuted for his crimes. In fact, his actions were not even crimes in the legal sense because no laws existed in Louisiana at that time to prevent the mistreatment of slaves. Perhaps that was due to the fact that most Southern state legislatures were made up of plantation owners, who wanted no infringements of any kind on their power, especially not when they were about to grab on to the ascending coattails of Southern independence and all the freedoms that it promised.

Manassas: True Pride/False Security

Far off on the northern Virginia "frontier," the rhetoric that had long fueled the drive toward that promised independence was dropping away and being replaced by the clang and rattle of an army digging in. By late July 1861, the Southern citizen-soldiers finally stood poised to meet the Yankees at a rail junction near Washington, D.C., called Manassas. Every regiment there contained braggarts, fools, and misinformed patriots, all of whom believed that the Confederacy would easily win the battle. And to both the glory and the eventual detriment of the entire South, that is exactly what happened.

After the smashing Confederate victory at the Battle of Manassas on July 21, the two principal commanders of the South, General

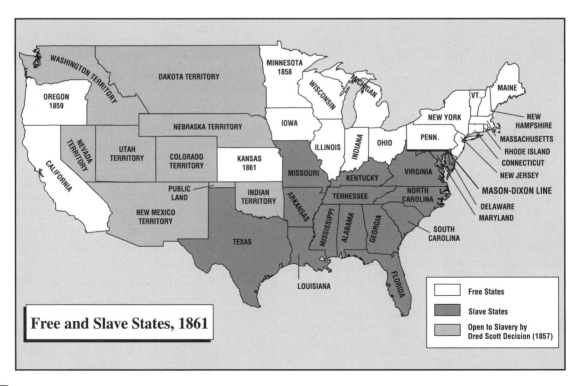

Free and Slave States, 1861

Free States

Slave States

Open to Slavery by Dred Scott Decision (1857)

Following the Confederate triumph at the Battle of Manassas, Rebel generals Joseph E. Johnston (left) and P. G. T. Beauregard (right) assured both their troops and the civilian population that a Southern victory was close at hand.

Joseph E. Johnston and General P. G. T. Beauregard, wanted to commend their men for the win. They issued a proclamation to be passed not only among the ranks but through the civilian population as well. Gushing forth praise and platitudes, the generals described how the outnumbered Rebels turned near defeat into grand victory and chased the Yankees from Southern soil.

The proclamation read:

It is with the profoundest emotions of gratitude to an overruling God, whose hand is manifest in protecting our homes and liberties, that we, your Generals commanding, are enabled, in the name of our whole country, to thank you for that patriotic courage, that heroic gallantry, that devoted daring, exhibited by you in the actions of the 21st, by which the hosts of the enemy were scattered, and a signal and glorious victory obtained.

Soldiers! We congratulate you on an event which ensures the liberty of our country. We congratulate every man of you, whose glorious privilege it was to participate in this triumph of courage and of truth—to fight in the Battle of Manassas. You have created an epoch in the history of liberty and unborn nations will rise up and call you "blessed."[20]

Reading sentiments such as these with their implied promise of a rapid victory in the war, it is no wonder that planters felt no need to begin altering the plantation lifestyle to meet the demands of a long-term war. Indeed, the top generals themselves were assuring them that the war was already won. And the next several months would not do much to dispel the accompanying notion that one Rebel was worth ten Yankees. So on it would go, the ancient Southern way of living, with every planter assuming that it would last forever and every lady taking heart at that prospect.

The Ladies Fair and Their Domain

Fort Sumter and Manassas were not the only Southern victories in 1861 that lulled the South into a false sense of security. Clear wins at Big Bethel near Richmond, Balls Bluff and Harpers Ferry in northern Virginia, and Wilson's Creek in southwestern Missouri also bolstered Confederate morale and fostered the sense that the Southern home front would escape radical upheaval. Even when the Southerners heard the news concerning Union gains in western Virginia, Maryland, and in the naval blockade, confidence in their own security still ran high. That being the case, even the fairest of fair ladies generally felt no threat to themselves or their plantations during the initial weeks of the war.

A Notable Exception

Mary Custis Lee, the wife of Confederate general Robert E. Lee and granddaughter of George Washington, lived in a large and beautiful estate in Arlington, Virginia. General Lee had left there when called to the Confederate capital at Richmond after Fort Sumter, and he had pleaded with her to follow him.

Reluctant to abandon her ancestral home, Mrs. Lee wrote to her husband, saying:

> I am very unwilling to do this; but Orton [a family friend] was so urgent and even intimated that the day was fixed for the Federals to take possession of our

Like many other Southern women, Mary Custis Lee (pictured) was confident that the Confederate army would stop the advancing Federal troops.

> heights. I believe they would like to have a pretext to invade.[21]

The Federals invaded even without a pretext just hours after Mrs. Lee had fled, eventually turning the mansion into an army headquarters and the grounds around it into a graveyard.

Birds in a Gilded Cage

For the most part, though, the traditional rhythms, roles, and responsibilities of plantation women remained unchanged throughout 1861, and the masters continued to dictate them based upon the contradictory social mores of the day. On the one hand, the men openly considered their wives to be inferior to them in practically every way and expected them to unquestioningly submit to their authority in all matters. On the other hand, they bathed their women in unconditional adoration and all-consuming love.

A Louisiana woman aptly summed up the paradox, writing:

In the typical upper-class Southern household the father and husband is the patriarch whose authority embraces his wife and children no less than his servants. The mother's role is a subordinate one. She is expected to be loving and properly submissive to her husband, to raise the children and look after their early education, to occupy the domestic sphere. Southern women are exalted in part to offset the disadvantages of their secondary status.[22]

Chivalry: A Two-Edged Sword

Manuals on etiquette and customs overflowed with rules not only defining how the exalted women should behave but how men should exalt them. Most of the injunctions had been handed down from the traditions of

Federal soldiers occupy Robert E. Lee's grand estate in Arlington, Virginia. The Federals turned the beautiful mansion into its army's headquarters and transformed the extensive grounds into a graveyard.

the English Cavaliers (who had previously adopted them from the knights and lords of the Middle Ages). The Cavaliers were stylish noblemen who had been defeated in the English civil war (1642–1648) by an army of Puritan commoners. To avoid beheading, many of the Cavaliers had fled to the sanctu-ary of the early Southern colonies, where they transplanted their ideals.

Central among those ideals was the notion of chivalry, the medieval code that placed honor above even life itself. A Scottish visitor observed that for offenses against a lady as seemingly insignificant as failing to

A Little Belle's Ball

Gentility, graciousness, and honor were the watchwords of the planter families: a spirit best summed up by the word *chivalry*. And there were few more legendary expressions of American chivalry than that of the South-ern ball. According to Lyle Saxon's *Old Louisiana*, one planter's young daughter remembered a ball this way:

> There were gorgeous costumes of real lace with jewels and plumes. The stair-case was garlanded with roses in all three flights. More flowers rested in vases on every mantel and bracket. Some gentlemen lost no time in swirling their ladies across the dance floor to the invigorating strains of white-gloved musicians. Other gentle-men discussed the matters of the day while sampling Scotch or Irish whiskey. Their ladies, dressed in magnificent gowns to the floor, chatted and laughed among themselves.

> About midnight supper was announced and the hostess led the way to the din-ing room. On the menu were cold meats, salads, salamis with galantines quaking in jellied seclusion, and an infi-nite variety of specialty dishes were served from side tables, leaving the expanse of carved oak silvered, linened, and laced. Flowers trailed from the tall

> silver vases in the center of the corsage bouquet at each place.

> Fruits and cakes stood in pyramids or layers or only solid deliciousness, iced and ornamented. Custards, pies, jellies, creams, Charlotte Russes or home-con-cocted sponge cakes spread with rasp-berry jams encircled a veritable Mont Blanc of whipped cream dotted with red cherry stars. Towers of nougat or caramel, sorbets and ice creams served in little baskets woven of candied orange peel and topped with sugared rose leaves or violets. There were vari-ous wines in cut glass decanters, each with its name carved in silver grapeleaf suspended from its neck and iced champagne deftly poured by the wait-ers into gold-traced or Bohemian glass-es. Wax candles in crystal chandeliers and in silver candelabra illuminated the whole. More dancing followed supper and went on all night long. At dawn, when the guests were leaving, a cup of strong black coffee and enchanting memories sustained them on the long carriage ride to their homes.

Events as Cinderella-like as these must have seemed in themselves worth going to war to preserve.

During the 1860s, plantation women submitted to the traditional, yet contradictory, roles of their gender. Southern men were expected to show the utmost respect for women, defending their reputations and showering them with unconditional adoration; however, these same men believed women were inferior and should submit to the authority of males.

bow, tip the hat, or yield on a sidewalk, the gentleman escorting that lady would

> call the offender out (to duel with pistols), and if he refused to come out, shoot him on sight. And for every man who was shot in a duel, a hundred were shot on sight, or stabbed in the heat of some unexpected quarrel.
>
> A Presbyterian minister, [he continued,] had an only sister, a widow, to whom a friend made "improper proposals." She informed her brother, who was 500 miles distant at the time. The clergyman rode the distance on horseback, found the offender and killed him. He was never prosecuted.[23]

Playing Knights and Damsels

Young plantation men often played out a somewhat less violent manifestation of chivalry in mock medieval tournaments, dressing up in knight's armor and jousting on

horseback with lances. Aside from the sheer thrill of risking serious injury, the reward for the victor was the honor of placing his fair maiden (in full damsel's dress) on a throne to be waited on by all the other costumed knights and ladies. Thus, the victorious knight would place the "queen of his heart" on a literal pedestal representing the figurative one on which she usually rested.

The following toast, offered at such social gatherings, further reinforced the belief that "maiden delicacy" supported the very foundation of Southern society: "To woman!!!" it went. "The center and circumference, diameter, and periphery, sine, tangent and secant of all our affections."[24]

Vulgar Women

What was a woman to do, though, in her mathematical majesty, at the glorious center of men's affection? Any activity that might induce perspiration was considered vulgar and any in the sun, potentially debasing. If it was even remotely possible that sunlight

Proper ladies aided the war effort by forming sewing circles and making uniforms for the Confederate soldiers.

would strike a lady on a short walk or a rowboat ride, she would have to be completely covered by a hat, long sleeves, ankle-length skirt, gloves, and a parasol. For nothing was more repulsive to a gentleman than a suntanned woman. Tans were for the poor unfortunates who had to labor in the sun for a living. Even more shocking, they might cause people to gossip about possible racial "impurities" in the lady's bloodline.

Even at Southern resorts where the men exhausted themselves through sports, for women, "there was no golf or tennis, not even the innocent croquet, to tempt her to athletics, so they drifted more to the 'Lydia Languish' style."[25] Reading, writing, studying, and reflecting—these male-approved, indoor activities were the only ones appropriate for true ladies. They made them better conversationalists at parties—and as such advanced their men's reputation and kept their skin alluringly pale. What could they do, then, to participate in the rising tide of patriotism that was sweeping them up as surely as it was the men? What could a proper lady do to aid the cause of Southern independence?

War Work Within the Bounds of Propriety

A few acceptable opportunities did arise during the initial months of the war for even the most genteel belles. Supervising the slaves' preparation of special meals for departing soldiers and distributing them at camps and train stations fell nicely within the parameters of ladyhood, as did the sewing of flags, socks, shirts, and uniforms. A smattering of work existed for comforting the few heroic wounded trickling home, writing letters for them and reading them novels, newspapers, and the Bible.

Judith Brockenbrough McGuire, a prominent Virginia matron, represented a great portion of Southern womanhood when she wrote:

> While men are making a free-will offering of their life's blood on the altar of their country, women must not be idle. We must do what we can for the comfort of our brave men. We must sew for them, knit for them, nurse the sick, keep up the faint-hearted, give them a word of

encouragement in season and out of season. There is much for us to do and we must do it!

Mrs. McGuire exhibited greater foresight than most overconfident Southerners did at the beginning of the war by adding:

The embattled hosts of the North will have the whole world from which to draw their supplies; but if, as it seems but too probable, our ports are blockaded, we shall indeed be dependent on our own exertions, and great must those exertions be.[26]

As pessimistic as many Confederates considered such predictions to be, unfolding events would prove them accurate.

Stepping Down from the Pedestal

As the plantation mistresses matured (or as more of their sons, husbands, brothers, and fathers volunteered for the army), they assumed greater responsibility around the plantation. The first work always entrusted to them centered around the manor houses and included the management of the domestic servants. That meant that they had to step down from the rarified air of their lofty pedestals and into the push-and-pull arena of practical authority and submission. Complicating the task, a tactful mistress had to always keep in mind that some of the servants beneath her had been forces in her husband's home long before she had.

Female volunteers comfort a dying soldier as he reads his final letter from home.

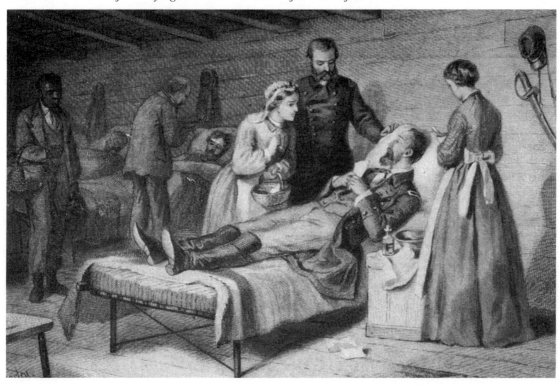

The workforces they had to direct could be considerable. Midsize mansions at the beginning of the Civil War typically had one butler, two parlor maids, a cook, four house-maids, one nursemaid, a washerwoman, one gardener, one coachman, and one seamstress for a total of at least thirteen servants. It was the mistress's responsibility to see that they had plenty of work to do, that they understood how to do it, and that they remained on the job until it was done.

The ladies also supervised the smoke-house, storehouse, dairy, and outside kitchen. Preparation of foodstuffs for the slaves and the family, medical care, and the manufacture and maintenance of all clothing might fall under their purview. But always the care and keeping of their homes ranked as the highest obligation.

The Big House

The manor house represented the very soul of plantation graciousness: family, society, tradition, honor, culture, business, pleasure, work, play, study, and life itself. Mary Chesnut perhaps captured the mystique of the plantation house most sublimely when she wrote:

> Mulberry Hill [her plantation near Columbia, South Carolina] is a watering-place where one does not pay, where there are no strangers, and where one day is curiously like another with people coming and going, carriages driving up or driving off.[27]

Though relatively few in number, the grand mansions of the Greek Revival style of

Fashioned in the Greek Revival style, this manor house is characteristic of the Southern plantation home.

Toilet paper was a relatively new phenomenon on the personal hygiene scene of the 1850s. The French had devised it some years before, but it had taken awhile for the design flaws to be worked out. Nevertheless, by the eve of the Civil War, the sanitary aid was catching on in Europe, but due to cost and availability, only the wealthy used it. All others had to continue using old scraps of cloth. Also, one candid writer reported, "newspapers or pages torn out of catalogs were used for toilet paper. And for reading."

Southern planters, never wanting to be too far out of step with the trend-setting French, began to import some of their *papier de toilet* but not in great quantities. Not only was it expensive and hard to find, but Southern users soon found out that the fabled tissue was not as effective as hoped. In fact, instead of being absorbent and soft, it tended to be rather slick and waxy, so most planter families continued with the old ways. Regardless of how much wealthy Southerners liked to think of themselves as being among the avant-garde, they always had been creatures of tradition and habit. Besides, once domestic war shortages and the naval blockade really hit them, they would be lucky to find broad leaves and de-kerneled corncobs that did not chafe.

architecture came to symbolize the Southern plantation home. Most boasted tall white columns befitting a state capitol building. Inside, oak and marble floors shone with the high gloss of one hundred hand buffings, and elegant staircases curved and spiraled upward as if to heaven itself.

Each of the twelve to fifteen large rooms had a high ceiling to allow the heat to rise above standing height on days when the Southern sun could wilt a watermelon. There were no closets built into the walls; unattached wardrobe furniture held coats and clothing. Manors were taxed according to their number of rooms and, to the tax man, built-in closets counted as rooms.

One contemporary account mentioned that

velvet-tasseled bell-pulls [inside doorbells attached to a cord hanging outside] announced guests. Upon passing through a set of high, double front doors, those guests usually entered into a wide hallway that ran all the way to the back of the house.[28]

The principal rooms were positioned through wide doorways to the right and left. These large parlor rooms were wallpapered with panoramic landscapes or historical scenes and contained Europe's finest chandeliers, portraits, and furniture (which might have included a circular sofa, corner-fit chair, a serpentine-back sofa, and, of course, a piano).

It was in these rooms that the planter and his mistress held their dances, the legendary balls and social events. At such times crystal punch bowls and lavish spreads of food filled the dining room (directly behind one of the front parlor rooms). Another well-appointed sitting room usually stood behind the other parlor. This was where the family spent its quiet evenings, reading, conversing, and relaxing among themselves. During parties, men retired there in their swallowtail coats to sip whiskey, smoke cigars, and speak privately about "masculine" matters.

The grand parlors of Southern mansions, lavishly decorated with fine European furniture, were the focal points of numerous gala events.

For Family Members Only

One planter's child remembered:

> The bedrooms upstairs all had canopied beds with fluffy, goose-feather mattresses and thick throw-rugs on the floors. As in every other room, draped windows reached nearly to the ceilings, letting in the main source of interior lighting: sunlight.[29]

Mirrors magnified the little light that made it in, the frames of which served as further ornamentation.

At night, candles and oil lamps provided some illumination and did so with a rich, golden glow. Thomas Webster's popular *Encyclopedia of Domestic Economy* recommended candles over oil lamps, stating:

> Candles supply the most convenient and the most general mode of obtaining artificial light for domestic purposes. Until lately, two substances only, wax and tallow, were known as material for candles; spermaceti [solidified whale oil] was next introduced, and at present various substances such as stearine [chemically enhanced animal fat] are added.[30]

Handy near every bed stood the ceramic chamber set, a large bowl with a wide-mouthed pitcher for washing, a cup for brushing the teeth, and a chamber pot enclosed in a wooden box with a toilet seat.

Since indoor plumbing was not yet in common usage, this pot eliminated the need for midnight sojourns to the two-holed privy way out in back. In the morning a servant emptied them out and scrubbed them spotless by hand. She would then replace the pot in its wooden box for use again that night.

These upstairs rooms might have contained a writing table (perhaps American Empire or Gothic Victorian style) with quill pens that had to be dipped in a bottle of ink every few words. There was often a three-way folding screen behind which to dress, a mirrored vanity, perhaps a Boston rocker or a straight-back chair, or a wooden rocking cra-

dle if there was a new baby in the home. The children's rooms usually had a toy chest or a rocking horse and perhaps a few toy guns or dolls. All bedrooms had to have brass bed warmers (which looked like covered copper skillets attached to broom handles). Servants filled them with hot coals from the fireplaces on cold, wintry nights and slipped them under the mattresses to heat them up.

A Room of Many Uses

There were no showers or built-in bathtubs so once or sometimes twice a week each family

Room, Books, and Board

Plantation mothers sent their boys off to boarding school at age eight or nine. The young gentlemen started out studying spelling, grammar, arithmetic, and geography. Even at academies not specifically geared toward military instruction, they were "formed into military corps for drill and discipline." Thus formed, they would be drilled for an hour a day before breakfast and attend mandatory prayers morning and evening. All students had to go to church on Sunday, where their instructors hoped to infuse them with what one planter father called a "living conviction of Moral Accountability." The younger boys probably also prayed to survive the traditional hazing doled out by the older upperclassmen (tacitly permitted by the faculty for additional "character-building" purposes).

As they advanced into their adolescent years, the boys chose a particular area of specialization. Those desiring to go into business as adults took courses in mathematics, penmanship, bookkeeping, and oth-

er commercial skills. Future engineers pursued geology, surveying, navigation, and civil engineering, while those designated to inherit their fathers' plantation learned agriculture, chemistry, mineralogy, and botany.

At finishing schools, young adolescent girls began a more rigorous program of study intended to reinforce their proficiency in the "Ornamentals" and the delicate arts of ladyhood. They received cotillion, etiquette, and dance classes in equal measure with those in literature, poetry, elocution, and music. One contemporary woman observed that educators

took for granted that women should be educated, though not trained for the professions, if they were to be the companions of educated men. Southern institutions were thus turning out a steady stream of accomplished individuals—doctors, lawyers, clerics, orators—and people who made a pastime of reading.

member stripped in the downstairs kitchen, stood in a round wooden or tin tub, and lathered up with a harsh lye soap while servants poured fire-heated water all over them. Attempts were made to provide the bather with privacy, but boys and girls growing up on plantations learned early about the distinctive differences between the human male and female. Living among breeding and birthing livestock also contributed to an early understanding of sexuality (though "proper" children were forbidden to discuss it).

Of course, the inside kitchen had culinary functions as well. Shining metal pots, pans, and specialized utensils for every food-related chore imaginable hung on the walls and cluttered the countertops. Very little food was actually cooked here, though, for fear of burning down the mansion. The hearth fires were kept sequestered outside in a separate kitchen, but, still, devastating fires were not uncommon.

The Fires of War Spread Southward

After the initial Confederate victories of 1861, several relatively quiet months passed during which it appeared that the plantation mistresses might never have more to worry about than kitchen fires. The year 1862 dispelled that myth, however, and hurled many plantation women directly into the gnashing teeth of three separate Union invasions.

Kate Cumming, age twenty-eight, lived in western Tennessee during the huge and gruesome Battle of Shiloh. She traveled to

The Seed Corn

Many a plantation mother turned over her boys (usually with some reluctance) to be trained up in the ways of the army. Early in the Civil War, such young cadets at the Virginia Military Institute and other Southern martial academies came to be referred to as "seed corn," implying that they should not be "eaten up" by frontline battling. Rather, it was thought, they should be "planted" among the civilian-soldiers for the higher purposes of training, motivating, and disciplining them. At the first guns of war, though, most cadets sixteen years old and older broke loose from the intolerable restraints of school and ran off to die as privates. The cadets, still too young to enlist, avoided this initial "spending of the seed corn" at least until the Southern army found itself desperate enough to call upon even them.

At the Battle of New Market, Virginia, the undermanned Confederate army hurled the V.M.I. cadets into Union lines, forcing the seasoned enemy to flee in terror from the field. The victory had its cost, however, as noted in the official battle report: "The fire was withering. It seemed impossible that any living creature could escape; and here we sustained our heaviest loss, a great many being wounded, and numbers knocked down, stunned, and temporarily disabled." The cadets won the battle, but due to their courage as frontline soldiers, few ever got the chance to be seeded as leaders. Not many grizzled Rebel veterans felt inclined to take orders from boys anyway, regardless of how much "book larnin'" they had.

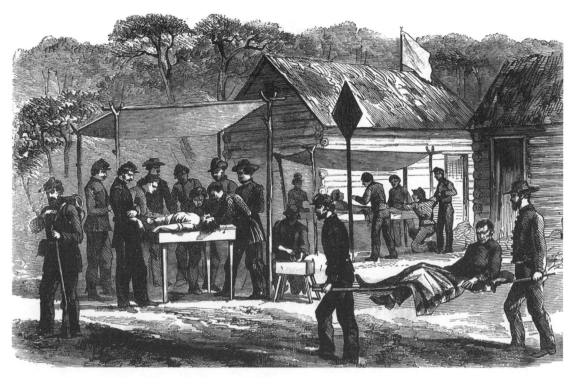

Surgeons tend to the wounded in a field hospital. In addition to military personnel, civilian volunteers provided invaluable assistance to injured soldiers.

the battlefield intending to give food to some of the thousands of Confederate casualties but ended up actually nursing them. Never having seen a wound worse than a cut finger, she entered a "hospital" and found the devil's own inferno. She wrote:

The men were lying all over the house on their blankets just as they were brought in from the battlefield. The air was foul with this mass of human beings. We had to walk and kneel in blood and water. There was much suffering. One old man groaned all the time. He had lost a leg. Another was wounded through the lungs and had a most excruciating cough and seemed to suffer awfully. One fine-looking man had a dreadful wound in the shoul-

der. I bathed it and he thanked me but he died before breakfast.[31]

After occupying New Orleans, Louisiana, federal ships sailed up the Mississippi River to Baton Rouge and bombarded the homes of civilians. An upper-class young lady by the name of Sarah Morgan recorded the scene around her mansion:

Bang! went a cannon and that was all our warning. Mother added her screams to the general confusion. Lilly gathered up her children who were crying hysterically all the time. Lucy saved the baby, naked as she took her from her bath, only throwing a quilt over her. The firing still continued. What awful screams! I heard

Miriam plead, Lilly shriek; the children screaming within; women running by without, crying and moaning. We took to the road. It was a heart-rending scene. Women were searching for their babies, where they had been lost in the flood of refugees; others were sitting in the dust, crying and wringing their hands.[32]

The people of Richmond, Virginia, received their first exposure to real war in June 1862. An immense Federal army advanced up the peninsula to within twenty miles of the capital, theatening to capture the entire city. Rebel forces managed to push them back but not before inundating the city with thousands upon thousands of horribly maimed casualties. One Southern lady reported, "Almost every house in the city became a private hospital and almost every woman a nurse." Society matrons and plantation mistresses cringed at the "awfully smashed-up objects of misery" but set about tending to their grotesque injuries anyway.[33]

A Rich Woman's War as Well?

Clearly, the vultures of war were beginning to roost around many Southern plantations. And yet any planter could avoid military service altogether if he (or his wife) desired it. In hopes of preventing slave uprisings and agricultural collapse, the Confederate government allowed all owners and overseers of twenty or more slaves to remain home to keep the plantations secure and productive. This "Twenty-Slave Law" eventually caused common Southerners to bitterly complain that the struggle for independence was "a rich man's war and a poor man's fight."[34]

During the Civil War, countless numbers of women were called upon to nurse wounded soldiers, both in their own homes and in army hospitals.

Nevertheless, for the plantation mistresses and their men, who were inclined to take advantage of the inequities, the good life continued. They lived comfortably in their "big houses" served by their domestic servants and craftsmen. And while these specialized workers lived far better lives than "lesser" slaves on the plantation, the gulf that existed between them and the "mista and missus" still equaled the differences between black and white.

The "Fortunate" Few

White planters were the first to recognize the value of their black slaves. One said, "The plantations and estates of this Province cannot be well and sufficiently managed and brought to use, without the labor and service of slaves."[35] Another added, "A Negro's life is too valuable to be risked. Do not, by attempting to do too much, over-work and consequently injure your hands. Do not kill the goose that lays the golden egg."[36]

The masters, however, considered some slaves to be more valuable to the plantation than others, and the blacks themselves came to accept that "pecking order." A black woman observed:

There was many classes 'mongst de slaves. De first class was de house servants. These was de butler, de maids, de nurses, chambermaids, an' de cooks. De next class was the carriage drivers and de gardeners, de carpenters, de barber, and de stable men. Then come de next class: de wheelwright, wagoners, blacksmiths, and slave foremen. De next class I remembers was de cow men and the niggers dat have care of de dogs. All these have good houses an' never have to work in de fields or git a real beatin'.[37]

Although this woman was not altogether correct about the beatings, she properly

A photograph taken in 1862 shows several generations of slaves on a South Carolina plantation.

The "Fortunate" Few   **35**

Child Labor

Practically as soon as the children of house servants could stoop, they began "paying off the master's investment." Little houseboys pulled weeds, fed chickens, scared crows away from the cornfields, and kept hawks from snatching up young turkeys. In any time left over, they carried meals and water to adult servants, hoed, tilled, and watered the garden, gathered eggs, swept porches, and hauled refuse to the compost heap.

Little house girls did not escape the workaday blues either. If anything, they had more responsibilities than their brothers. They had to milk the cows (because that task was considered too "unmanly" for even a slave boy to do) and feed all the stock animals. Inside the mansion, house girls worked in the nursery, ensuring, among other things, that the babies always had a fresh cut of fat bacon to suck on as a pacifier. In addition, they made beds, churned butter, mopped floors, shooed flies, and emptied chamber pots.

A particularly funny or personable houseboy or house girl might escape the more onerous chores by simply assuming the unofficial role of household pet. These "lucky" boys and girls could even be assigned the permanent job of entertaining the planter children.

But regardless of where they fit into the occupational hierarchy, whether at the top or the bottom, all slave boys and girls could count on one irrevocable thing: They would be spending the rest of their lives toiling ceaselessly without pay and never, ever be allowed to leave.

identified the class strata within the plantation's black population and the people who occupied the "upper" and "middle" classes.

Butlers: The Other Gentlemen

No positions within the slave hierarchy held any more "prestige" than those of the house servants, and the senior male member among them was the butler. This seniority should not suggest that the "gentleman's gentleman" lived an easy life or that he would have remained in his elite job if offered his freedom. It does, however, mean that he received better food, clothing, shelter, and working conditions while passing his time in captivity. In return for these perquisites, the master expected this "lucky" slave to speak proper English, exhibit impeccable etiquette, and keep his appearance neat at all times while carrying out all the normal duties of a personal servant.

Along with these obligations also came a great deal of responsibility for the performance of the other domestic servants, and this authority was sometimes as much a curse as a blessing. Few young men ever held this position simply because of the many years of apprenticeship required to master the subtleties of peer management, and, respect or not, many apprentices considered the burden of leadership too oppressive to bear.

Since the planter and his wife considered it a gross humiliation when any of their house servants fumbled over their duties (especially in the presence of guests), the butler could expect to feel the owner's wrath when any of the house servants committed an infraction. Rarely did that mean a full whipping, but a slap across the face or a switching to the legs with a riding crop was not uncommon for even the most senior of errant slaves.

A butler presents his masters with the Thanksgiving turkey. In the slave hierarchy, a butler was the most prestigious and powerful of all the domestic servants on the plantation.

To avoid that kind of punishment, the butler had to insure that all those under him (maids, waiters, apprentices, houseboys, and house girls) politely provided every possible service required of them by family members and guests (regardless of how inconsiderate they might be). If they did, those servants would be able to share the sentiments of one well-trained, white-haired gentleman's gentleman, who said proudly, "The house servants and butler in particular was what the Master and the Missus called a 'different class.'"[38] But if the servants failed in any way, the supervising butler as well as the offending domestics would have to be "reeducated" or, worse, sent down to the cotton fields and forgotten.

Mammies: The Other Mothers

Butlers were not the only senior servants from whom more was expected and more

exacted. Mammies, the top black women in the house, also understood that if they did not want to end up picking cotton, they had better learn (and teach others) to defer to the judgment of their immediate boss: the master's wife. And the mistress's judgment could often be faulty, especially if she was young or newly married. Consequently, experienced mammies who possessed more knowledge than the mistress concerning children, medicine, and life in general would often pretend to know less than the master's wife in her presence while furtively doing what she knew was best behind her back.

One mistress, Mary Bateman, watched her daughter's health deteriorate in spite of giving her a "modern" prescription prepared by the local physician. She refused the mammy's request to make her own medicine from herbs and roots, calling it "voodoo" and "superstition"—but the mammy brewed and administered the concoction anyway. After the girl made a "miraculous" recovery, the servant told the mistress what she had done. Mrs. Bateman eventually conceded that the "superstitious" mammy had probably saved her daughter's life and repaid her with a permanent and appreciated place in the household.

Although mammies often had a broad understanding of the healing arts, the principal tasks assigned to them usually involved the rearing of planter children and, if they had recently given birth themselves, they might begin their responsibilities as wet nurses. As such, they actually fed the suckling planter baby with their own mothers' milk (a process considered beneath a cultured white mother). One former wet nurse, when asked in her old age if she had any children, claimed that she had "'bout two thousand and most all of them be white."[39]

Once the infant was weaned, the mammy provided all aspects of the child's practical

A slave child looks on as a mammy lulls one of the planter's children to sleep. Mammies were usually the senior female slaves on the plantation and were responsible for rearing the master's children.

mothering. Those tasks included, but were not limited to, bathing, rocking, feeding, burping, dressing, entertaining, walking, guiding, disciplining, chiding, hugging, consoling, kissing, bandaging, teaching, and generally nurturing the child. She would sometimes begin the process all over again for the first child's offspring and, as a white-haired ancient, for the grandchildren as well. It is not surprising that the planter's sons and daughters often felt closer to their mammies than anyone else in the family or that the mammy's status around the home many times rivaled that of blood relatives.

Maids and the Mundane

Another coveted yet considerably less favorable position in the slave hierarchy was that of maid. Maids, then as now, performed whatever household tasks around the mansion that

their mistresses demanded, such as cleaning, straightening, mopping, waxing, dusting, carpet beating, and serving tea and light meals. Some maids escaped the worst of that domestic drudgery by being assigned to a particular family member. A former mistress's maid recalled her duties in the following way:

> Cook? No, ma'am! And I never washed, never washed so much as a rag. All I washed was my mistress' feet. I was a lady's maid. I'd wait on my mistress. When she would sleep, it was my duty to fan her with fans made out of turkey feathers, feather fans. Part of it was to keep her cool and part of it was to keep the flies off. I remember how I couldn't stomp my feet to keep the flies from bitin' me, for fear of wakin' her up.[40]

It is clear that many of the "high-class" servants were subject to as much demeaning condescension and humiliating work as were the field hands. In fact, this was sometimes multiplied for the house servants simply because they had to spend so much time beneath the watchful eye of their taskmasters.

This prompted one former maid to complain:

> We was constantly exposed to the whims and passions of every member of the family; from the least to the greatest their anger was wreaked upon us. Nor was our life an easy one, in the hours of our toil or in the amount of labor performed. We was always required to sit up until all the family had retired; then we must be up at early dawn in summer, and before day in winter.[41]

And these jobs represented some of the best that slavery had to offer. Only one position reigned more supreme.

The Cook: Unfettered yet Still Unfree

The cook enjoyed the greatest respect, if not fear, from the mistress and all the slave elite, and she did not have to endure the close proximity to a meddling supervisor. The kitchen itself did not invite guests, especially

Planter children often felt a great affinity with the mammies who nurtured and cared for them from birth to adulthood.

those who wanted to remain free from smoke and heat. It was a little harder to reach, too, since it stood outside in a separate cabin (to prevent any possible fires there from spreading to the mansion).

One former cook remembered:

It wasn't built onto de big house. It be at the end of a big porch dat go from it to de big house. It had a great big fire place dat stretched most all de way 'cross one end of dat kitchen, and it had racks and cranes for de pots and pans and ovens. It even had a cookstove, a real sho 'nuff iron cookstove.[42]

Another cook on a different plantation recalled:

Our kitchen stood apart from de big house. I never seen such a big one. The sticks of wood for the fireplace was twelve feet long. There was hooks all around, two big hooks up in de chimney.

The cook wielded unparalleled power in the kitchen. Most plantation mistresses knew better than to interfere with matters pertaining to the kitchen or the cook's preparation of food.

They hung lambs and calves' hind quarters up in that chimney to smoke. The sweetest stuff you ever ate in your life![43]

Even though the mistresses theoretically had authority over the kitchen and all its workers, most learned at an early age to refrain from offering much advice regarding the preparation of the food.

One cook with twelve years of experience actually denied her new mistress access to the kitchen on more than one occasion (an insolence punishable by whipping if committed by any other servant). Once, she angrily rebuked the lady of the mansion, demanding, "Go into de house, Miss Carrie! You ain't no manner or use in here only to git yer face red with de heat! I'll have dinner like you wants it! Just read yer books an' rest easy till I sends it to yer dining room!"[44] At that final insult, the uninitiated mistress stormed to her husband and demanded that he remove the cook from her position. He laughed and said that he would be a fool to give up the best cook in the county on account of his wife's petty slights.

On yet another plantation, the cook's young daughter spoke right up when the mistress attempted to scold her mother. The little girl sassed, "Don't you scold my mammy 'bout de sorry way she done clean de chitlins! Don't you know mammy is boss of dis here kitchen. You can't come a fussin' in here!"[45] This mistress chose not to punish the girl or her mother for a simple reason—the cook was far too valuable an asset to the household to risk making her unhappy.

The Master's Middle Class

Carriage drivers, gardeners, carpenters, barbers, stable men, wheelwrights, wagoners,

Mmm . . . Mmm . . . Good!

Plantation families continued to eat well during the early months of the Civil War. It was still a time of economic prosperity, and the dinner table reflected that. The standard fare included many of the same foods we eat today, but there were some regional favorites as well, like stuffed hog intestines (better known as chitlins), hoecakes, collard greens (boiled kale leaves), corn pone, hominy grits, turnips, and black-eyed peas.

On rare occasions when all the children had been good, the mistress might have the cook serve up a special delight: boiled calf's head. A recipe book of the day, cited in Marc McCutcheon's Everyday Life in the 1800s, *described its preparation this way.*

"The calf's head should be cleansed with very great care; particularly the lights [the eyes, for they were to be eaten, too]. The head and the lights should boil two full hours. It is better to leave the windpipe on, for if it hangs out of the pot while the head is cooking, all the froth will escape through it. The brains, after thoroughly washed, should be put in a little bag, with one cracker, or as much crumbled bread, seasoned with sifted sage, and tied up and boiled one hour. After the brains are boiled, they should be well broken up with a knife and peppered, salted, and buttered."

blacksmiths, butchers, coopers, candlers, spinners, weavers, soap makers, gunsmiths, metalworkers, potters, basket weavers, tanners, cobblers, masons, painters, and slave drivers represented just a few of the possible occupations for slaves in the "middle class."

Innocence Gained and Lost

Children of the house servants and children of the master grew up practically as siblings. The same wet nurses fed them, the same mammies raised them, and the same butlers chased them out of the house when their bare feet were tracking in mud.

The boys stole away to fish in the rivers and catch frogs in the marsh; they sword-fought with sticks for sabers. Black and white, arm in arm, they climbed trees and built fortresses of dirt. They shot cows in the udder with slingshots. The girls played house and held elegant tea parties freely attended by blacks. They shared the same cups and took turns serving each other. All the young ladies got a turn as hostess.

By midchildhood, however, the relationships began to change. In make-believe adventures, only the white boys now emerged victorious with their trusted "servants" a few dutiful steps behind. And at the more realistic tea parties, the planter's girls always hosted while the black girls silently served.

The one-time friends separated thereafter, the whites to attend boarding schools and the blacks to go to work. And with each subsequent visit those differences grew, until the joyful friendships of childhood fossilized into the "proper" master-servant relationships, with only an occasional stolen smile to acknowledge a past warmly remembered by both.

While the full complement of these specialists was never assembled on a single plantation, any group of one hundred estate slaves could have been expected to include between fifteen and twenty of them. By most owners' admissions, these artisans kept the plantation from falling apart by repairing, replacing, and creating anew everything required for a secluded and self-supporting country estate.

The gardeners tended the landscaping, the carpenters constructed wooden buildings, the barbers cut hair and pulled teeth. Stable men groomed horses, wheelwrights made wagon wheels, wagoners drove wagons and cared for the oxen. Blacksmiths sweated over red-coaled fires, hammering out everything metal from horseshoes to nails; butchers killed hogs, pigs, calves, and cattle, and cut their hanging carcasses into meat.

Coopers made barrels, candlers dipped candles, spinners spun yarn for the weavers; tanners cured cowhide and cut it into leather, which cobblers pounded into shoes. Masons cemented stones to make walls, painters kept the buildings looking fresh, slave drivers insured that the field hands worked hard, and carriage drivers drove the planters wherever they wanted to go.

Even with their skills, these craftsmen endured long, physically strenuous hours. They labored, sweat, and sometimes slept in a collection of rough cabins behind the big house. Most lived grimy, dirty lives due to the nature of their work and never mastered the white man's manners or grammar.

As a result, they did not command the same respect throughout the plantation as did the more socially adept house servants. However, since the master considered them indispensable to the maintenance of the estate, they enjoyed considerably more freedoms and privileges than the field hands.

Carriage Drivers

The carriage driver considered himself to be more valuable than the other skilled servants because he had been trained how to act in the presence of white people. One such driver by the name of Ben Chambers apprenticed himself into his prestigious position at an early age, and even as a free man, he never stopped being proud of it. He described himself as "kinda like the vice-president of the plantation" and boasted of his service to his master.

When not caring for the magnificent steeds in the stable or driving them in his white gloves, top hat, and tails, he shined and spit polished the carriages daily as if they might be summoned to an important social engagement

The house servants held a higher rank than the middle-class craftsmen, even though both of these classes of slaves were considered superior to the field hands and enjoyed relatively comfortable lifestyles.

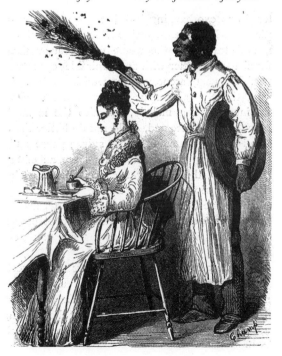

at any moment. Smiling toothlessly in old age, he remembered his slave days with a glimmer of nostalgia, saying, "That was the bestest of all the jobs on de plantation. Back then some niggers was sorta jealous of me."[46]

Slave Drivers

Slave drivers earned their respect and envy in quite another way; they demanded it through strength and intimidation. Drivers were usually of an

> imposing physical presence capable of commanding obedience from the other slaves. Ex-slaves described the drivers variously as, "a great big colored man," "a large tall, black man," "a burly fellow . . . severe in the extreme." Armed with a whip and outfitted in high leather boots and greatcoat, all emblematic of plantation authority, the driver exuded an aura of power.[47]

Even with all those advantages, being a slave driver had its drawbacks. He had to rise before the field hands and go to bed after they did while continually exhibiting all the characteristics the master expected from a driver. He had to work hard, demonstrate a sound knowledge and application of farming techniques, master white English, and maintain the respect of his fellow slaves. If he failed to perform any of these tasks, the white overseer or the master would return him to field work alongside some understandably bitter, grudge-holding hands.

Butchers

Butchers did not make nearly as many enemies as slave drivers, but their "privileged duties" were equally noxious (being bloody and smelly). Joseph Holmes, reporting on his plantation butchering days, said:

> Now you asked about hog-killin' time? Dat was de time of times. For weeks, us men would haul wood an' big rocks, an' pile 'em together as high as a house and then have several piles like that 'round a big hole in the ground that was filled with water. Then, us would start that pile of wood on fire and then start knockin' them hogs in the head. Us always used an axe. After knockin' the hog in the head, knockin' them out but not killin' them right off, us wanted to keep their hearts beatin' after we cut 'em to pump the blood out, you know. Then us would tie a rope on his leg, and after the water got to the right heat from them red-hot rocks, the hog would be throwed in it an' drug around awhile, then taken out to get its guts cut out and the rest cut up into sections and hung up in the smokehouse. Lawsie, we used to have sho'-'nuf meat then![48]

A Field Hand's View

The various craftsmen and -women supplied nearly every need of the plantation. They had to. Most plantations spread across miles and miles of unpopulated land, and no towns or stores existed near enough to provision them. One field hand by the name of Charley Williams marveled at the self-sufficiency the "middle-class" slaves provided, saying:

> Any plow gits broke, it goes to de blacksmith nigger. Then the anvil starts danglin' in de blacksmith shop—"Tank! Deling-ding! Tank! Deling-ding!"—and dat old bull tong gittin' straightened out!

'Course you can't hear de shoemaker awling and pegging, and de card spinners, and de old mammy sewin' by hand, but maybe you can hear de old loom going, "frump, frump" and you know it all right iffen your clothes be wearin' out, 'cause you going to git new britches purty soon!

> We had about a hundred niggers on dat place, young and old. We could make about every kind of thing, 'cepting coffee and gunpowder that our white folks and us needed. All cloth 'cepting Mistress' Sunday dresses come from de sheep to de carders to de spinners and de weaver. Then they dye it with "butternut" and hickory bark and indigo and other things and it set with copperas [copper water]. Leather be tanned on de place to make shoes, and I never see a store-bought wagon wheel, 'cepting among de stages and de freighters on de big road.

> There was them that made purty, long back-combs out'n cow horn and knittin' needles out'n hickory and carpenters that split young hickory and made it into wagons and rockin' chairs and such. It was just like that till I was growed, and then one day come a neighbor man and say we in war.[49]

Another Field Hand's View

It would be some time before that war actually reached most plantations, and longer still before it freed the majority of the slaves. In the meantime, the house servants and craftsmen would continue their relatively comfortable lifestyles. Those comforts, however,

Field hands plant sweet potatoes on a South Carolina plantation in 1862. Although field hands were at the bottom of the slave hierarchy, it was their hard physical labor that kept the plantation running.

tended to isolate them from the field hands, from 80 percent of their black brothers and sisters, and caused them to be resented and distrusted. In fact, many skilled slaves were pressured by their owners to report crimes, runaways, and insurrection plots, causing one field hand to report:

> Many of them house niggers is the most despicable tale-bearers and mischief-makers. They'll betray their fellow slave to get the favor of the massa an' by tattlin' get the nigger severely whipped; an' for these acts of spyin' he gets rewarded by the massa, who knows it is for his interest to keep such ones about him; though he is sometimes obliged to send the tattler away for fear of the vengeance of the betrayed slaves.[50]

This apparent loyalty to the master revealed itself in another significant way. Few house servants or craftsmen ever attempted to run away or exploit the considerable freedom they had to move about.

Such was not the case, however, for the mass of common field hands. They possessed neither the skills nor the talents needed to achieve the "good life" around the plantation. Most of them would spend their lives without even getting as far as the porch of the big house.

Yet the planters themselves would have been the first to admit that it was the field hands' strong backs and glacial endurance that made the plantation system work. And that explains why they went to such great lengths to keep the "talentless" field hands securely locked in the cellar of the plantation hierarchy.

The Muscle That Made the Money

Field hands made up three-quarters of the four million black men and women in bondage. They existed at the lowest level of the plantation system, generally either despised, pitied, or patronized by everyone in and around the manor house from the master down to the least skilled of all the craftsmen. Even barefooted houseboys considered themselves better than these human beasts of burden and no self-respecting person of any class or color would have considered for a moment working the way that they did.

A Day in the Life

Field work included plowing, hoeing, planting, harvesting, pulling fodder, digging ditch-

Field hands tote their hoes in from the fields after a long day of work. During the hoeing season, slaves worked grueling twelve-hour workdays cultivating their master's fields.

Working for the Weekend

Saturday night square dances provided the best chance for slaves to "lay their burdens down." Drawn to the music of banjos, spoons, washboards, and guitars made from gourds, they gathered excitedly in dirt-floored barns or warehouses to forget, if only for an evening, that they were slaves. Men laughed, women jigged, everyone do-si-doed. Loosened up by liquor, they clapped their hands, stomped their feet, and sang out to the heavens above.

Both the planter and the slaves realized the temporary benefit provided by a few jugs of whiskey at a dance. Cordelia Thomas, a little girl at the time, observed:

They stopped so often to swig that corn liquor Master provided for them that before midnight folks started fallin' out and droppin' down in the middle of the dance ring. The others would get 'em by the heels and drag 'em off to one side, till they come to and was ready to drink more liquor and dance again. That was the way they went on till daybreak.

Monday morning always followed the weekend, though, and often drained away even the memory of the good times. For the slaves knew that, as always, they would have to endure another five and a half excruciating workdays before they would be able to dance again.

---

es, chopping down trees, sawing timbers, clearing away foliage, splitting rails, constructing stone walls and fences, hauling rocks, pulling out stumps, and picking worms off of plants. And regardless of which of these travails the field hands might be assigned on any given day, they could be sure that day would begin early and end late.

The hoeing season began in April, just after the planting of cotton seeds, and required a "mere" twelve-hour workday. From "can to can't" (can see to can't see), men and women stooped over with their hoes, dug at the ground, and repeatedly bent down to pick up any old roots and branches from the previous year's growth. On hot days, they sweat. On cold days, they shivered. And every day the muscles in their arms, legs, and backs burned with strains, cramps, and aches. But, as nagging as those problems were, they were not among the most serious.

One woman field hand wrote:

During all these hoeings, the fastest hoer took the lead row. He usually about a rod in advance of his companions. If one of them pass him, he is whipped. If one fall behind or is a moment idle, he is whipped. In fact, the lash be flying from mornin' till night, the whole day long. This continues thus from April until July, a field havin' no sooner been finished than another is commenced.[51]

As dreadful as the hoeing season must have been, the August picking season was worse. Not only was the work harder and the sun hotter, it caused more pain because the coarse raw cotton made the pickers' fingers bloody and sore. And each of those picking days lasted eighteen full hours, from approximately 6:00 A.M. until midnight. By the time

the slaves could finally drag themselves back to their cabins and collapse into bed, it would often be 2:00 A.M., leaving just three hours of unconsciousness before having to get up and do it all over again.

Homes and Hovels

The homes where the field hands snatched those few hours of sleep usually stood less than a mile away from the manor house complex but the distance between the two population centers might just as well have been infinite. It was understood that the lice-infested, sweat-wreaking field hands were to remain in or around their own rudely constructed one-room dwellings without venturing far from their muddy squalor. They were

(Above) Slaves worked extremely long hours during the picking season, staying in the cotton fields from 6:00 A.M. to midnight. (Below) Field hands congregate near a run-down slave hut. Crude quarters like this greatly contrasted with the opulence of the manor house.

Two slave families were often forced to live together in one-room log cabins. These wretched huts were poorly constructed and quickly became overcrowded and filthy.

practically under house arrest in the dirt-floored, drafty, and overcrowded log huts they called "home."

One slave said:

> The cabins was cheap built. There wasn't no money spent on them. There wasn't even no nails used in the buildin'. The spaces between the logs was only covered with mud and straw. The benches and tables and bunks was put together with wooden pegs.[52]

For heat and cooking, the slaves built mud-and-stick hearths and chimneys. Keeping a fire going in the drafty cabins had its drawbacks, though. One slave noted that "the wind and rain will come in and the smoke will not go out."[53] They would heat up, however, creating yet another problem: infestations of cockroaches, lizards, snakes, and frogs, all in search of a little warmth.

Although the average slave cabin housed two families, even the better brick or clapboard ones were no larger than ten feet by ten feet and sometimes had no windows to let in sunshine or fresh air. A former field hand remembered, "They had no light but what was admitted by the open door or the cracks between the logs."[54] Charles Dickens, on a visit to America, simply called the slave quarters that he saw "very crazy, wretched cabins."[55]

The Bill of Fare

In some cases, what they ate inside those cabins was no less wretched. Field hand Solomon Northrup, who belonged to a rather miserly planter, subsisted on the "corn and

Slave Labor

The following three slave accounts from Julius Lester's To Be a Slave *describe the phases of a typical workday during picking season. The punishments varied depending upon the planter, but the work itself remained constant throughout the South.*

"[In the morning] each slave is presented with a sack. A strap is fastened to it, which goes over the neck, holding the mouth of the sack breast high, while the bottom nearly reaches to the ground. Each one is also presented with a large basket that will hold about two barrels. This is to put the cotton in when the sack is filled. The baskets are carried to the field and placed at the beginning of the rows. When the sack is filled, it is emptied into the basket and trodden down. . . .

[From midday until nightfall], with the exception of ten or fifteen minutes which is given us at noon to swallow our allowance of cold bacon, we are not permitted to be a moment idle until it is too dark to see, and when the moon is full, we often times labor until the middle of the night. We do not dare to stop even at dinnertime, nor return to the quarters, however late it be, until the order to halt is given by the driver. . . .

[When the day's work was over in the fields of a less gracious planter], the baskets is 'toted,' or in other words, carried to the gin house an' weighed. No matter how weary he may be, no matter how much he longs for sleep and rest, a slave never approach the gin house with his basket of cotton but with fear. If it fall short in weight, if he has not done the full task before him, he know that he must suffer. And if he has gone over by ten or twenty pounds, his master will measure the next day's task by that amount. It was rare that a day passed without one or more whippings. This occurred at the time the cotton was weighed."

bacon" diet, where the two principal ingredients were "given out at the corn crib and smoke-house every Sunday morning." For the entire week, Northrup wrote,

> All that was allowed was three and a half pounds of bacon, and corn enough to make a peck of meal [ground-up corn]. That is all—no tea, coffee, sugar, and with the exception of a very scanty sprinkling now and then, no salt.[56]

Not many recipes existed for cooking the precious bacon. Slaves just fried it and used the grease for seasoning. The cornmeal, however, lent itself well to creative cookery, and some popular dishes evolved. Mixed with cold water and a little salt (when available), cooks made a variety of corn breads: ashcake covered with hot ashes, johnnycake fried in a griddle, and sloosh (cornmeal saturated with grease and skewered over an open flame to cook).

Many times, there was seldom enough of any dish to fully feed a family, so slaves fished in nearby streams for extra food. Whatever they could manage to catch was often all that might assuage their own and their children's gnawing hunger pangs from one week to the next. Even when they could trap a squirrel or a rabbit, that hunger never completely subsided. Some slaves complained of spending all their days with a rumbling stomach and a nagging preoccupation with food. Others reported recurring dreams about it, only to wake up frustrated and even hungrier.

One field hand recalled, "We had a pretty hard time to make out and was hungry lots of times. Marse Tom [his master] didn't feel called on to feed his hands any too much. I had a cravin' for victuals all the time."[57] Those cravings sometimes drove the slaves to steal food from the kitchen and big house. There were cooks who surreptitiously fed them, too. Either way, if caught, all involved would suffer varying degrees of punishment, depending on the master's style.

The Clothes on Their Backs

A more immediate problem than either shelter or food existed for some field hands.

Their inadequate or nonexistent clothing exposed them to cold, heat, sickness, and humiliation. The following slave account presents a poignant portrait of what sweat, grime, hard work, and substandard cloth could do to a field hand's wardrobe. On this particular plantation, it is obvious that the owner concerned himself very little with the comfort, health, or dignity of his "property," even though his neglect no doubt reduced the amount of work they could do for him.

The slave recalled one typical dawn this way:

> More than half of the gang (of 168) was entirely naked. Several young girls who had arrived at puberty, wearing only the

This painting from 1888 aptly portrays the attire of two elderly field hands during the Civil War era.

covering that nature had ornamented them with, and a great number of lads of equal or superior age, appeared in the same custom. There was neither bonnet, cap, nor headdress of any kind amongst us, except the old straw hat that I wore. Some of the men had old shirts and some ragged trousers, but no one wore both. Amongst the women several wore petticoats and many had shifts. Not one of the whole number wore both of these vestments.[58]

Extreme cases such as this one notwithstanding, there are many more reports of slaves who were dressed adequately. The slave quoted here describes typical slave clothing this way:

Our dress was of tow cloth [coarse homespun]; for the children nothing but a shirt; for the older ones a pair of pantaloons or a gown in addition, according to the sex. Beside these, in the winter, a round jacket or overcoat, a wool hat, once in two or three years, for the males, and a pair of coarse shoes once a year.[59]

A Kinder, Gentler Slavery?

Although the owning of another human being should be universally condemned, some research indicates that the majority of slaves led less desperate lives. During the 1930s, the federal government commissioned writers to interview former slaves and record

Depictions of slaves happily dancing and relaxing, like this one, suggest that life was often pleasant for slaves. During the 1930s, a government study found that 70 percent of the slaves they interviewed had positive recollections of their time on the plantations.

"De Devil's Own Hosses"

Young black men sometimes absconded during the night to rendezvous with girlfriends on other plantations, and they usually returned before dawn without anyone being the wiser. Those less fortunate, though, often came face-to-face with marauding horsemen paid by the masters to round up runaways. They were called pattyrollers, and absentees feared them mortally.

Even tolerant owners allowed the pattyrollers to punish the runaways severely, wanting to make an example of the runaways for the rest of the slaves without having to make themselves appear to be "the bad guys." The absentee's first capture merited thirty-nine lashes with a rawhide whip—the "black snake," as terrified victims called it. And with every subsequent capture, the number of lashes increased.

"The pattyrollers was always hangin' around at night," a slave girl said, to catch the niggers that was visiting away from their own plantations. Pattyrollers couldn't whip a nigger that had a pass, but they surely could one that didn't and the niggers got tired of askin' Old Master for passes every night, so they just lit out anyway and took what lashin' they got.

Another former field hand quoted in Elizabeth Silverthorne's *Plantation Life in Texas* remembered the pattyrollers with a song:

> Over de hill and down de holler
> Pattyroller ketch nigger by de collar
> Dat nigger run, dat nigger flyin'
> Run nigger run, dey give you thirty-nine

"I declare to goodness," he added after singing the verse, "pattyrollers was de Devil's own hosses."

---

their reminiscences for posterity. In the published study *Slave Narratives: A Folk History of Slavery in the United States from Interviews with Former Slaves*, more than 70 percent of the blacks interviewed reported dominantly positive recollections of their time in captivity. Some went so far as to say that their slave days had actually been among the happiest and most secure of their lives.

Issam Morgan of Mobile, Alabama, said of his owner:

Any time a slave worked overtime or cut more wood than he was supposed to, Massa pay him money for it, 'cause when ever us slaves seen somthin' we like, we did just like the white folks does now. Us bought it. Massa never whupped none of his slaves. None of his slaves ever run away. They all knowed they was well off. The Yankees offered me a hoss iffen I would go north with them, but I just couldn't leave the Massa even though I wanted that hoss mighty bad.[60]

Mary Rice, also of Alabama, stated this about her owners:

Massa Cullen an' Mistis Mary Jane was the best master and mistress in the world. Once when I was awful sick, Mistis Mary Jane had me brung in the Big House and put me in a room that sat on the other side of the kitchen so she could

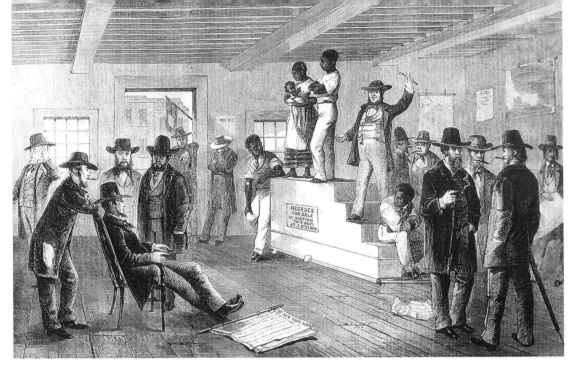

A family of slaves waits to be sold during a public slave auction in Virginia. In some auctions, slaves were placed on display in the nude and underwent degrading examinations by potential buyers.

take care of me herself 'cause I had to be nursed day and night. I was happy all the time in slavery days, but there ain't much to get happy over now.[61]

Arkansas field hand D. Davis said:

The first of every week, the Massa give each and every single man or family a task for the week and after that task is done they is through work for that week and can then tend the patches he give them to raise what they want on, an' what the slave raises on them patches would be theirs whatsosever it would be, cotton or taters, they own and they could sell it for money for them slaves to buy whatever they want.[62]

Alabamian Simon Phillips commented, "People has the wrong idea of slave days. We was treated good. My Massa never laid a hand on me the whole time I was with him. Sometimes we loaned the Massa money when he was hard pushed."[63]

Black children sometimes received special treatment from the mistress, as reported by Miulie Evans of North Carolina.

Every time Old Mistress thought we little black children was hungry 'tween meals she would call us up to the house to eat. Sometimes she would give us johnnycake and plenty of buttermilk to drink with it. It was so good. Every evenin' at three o'clock Old Mistress would call all us litsy bitsy children in, and we would lay down on pallets an' go to sleep. I can hear her singin' to us now.[64]

"My mammy and daddy," Harriet Payne proudly declared,

belonged to Colonel Jesse Chaney, much of a gentleman, and his wife, Miss Sallie, was the best mistress anybody ever had. We was fed good an' had plenty of clothes to keep us dry and warm. If all slaves had belonged to white folks like ours, there wouldn't have been no freedom wanted.[65]

An Alternative to the Auction Block

While most planters bought and sold slaves over the course of their careers, many at least attempted to make that potentially wrenching process as bearable as possible for the blacks. Some avoided the public auction blocks altogether, with their degrading nudi-ty and insensitive examinations, preferring to transact sales with neighbors and traders with proven reputations for benevolence.

A Texas planter by the name of Jared Groce sometimes lost money in his commit-ment to keeping families together. He once purchased a neighbor's crippled field hand, a man whom he knew he would have to sup-port until his death, so that his housemaid, the crippled man's bride, could live with her new husband. It was also Groce's practice (and that of many other Southern planters) to free his old, crippled, or infirmed slaves and allow them to live on his plantation fully cared for. He would even pull younger slaves away from their profit-generating tasks in order to have them take care of the "retirees" for as long as they needed it.[66]

A Steal at Any Price

Sales could be made suddenly, and the slave being sold often had little time to react. The very last to hear the news, however, were usually the family members, especially the mother and father. The reason was obvious. Breaking up a family created a furor every time that it happened. To avoid ugly scenes, the slave being bought would be grabbed quickly and spirited away unbeknownst to the rest of his or her family. In Elizabeth Silverthorne's Plantation Life in Texas, *for-mer house girl Mary Ferguson was quoted saying of her abduction.*

"About the middle of the evenin', up rode my young master on his hoss, an' up drive two strange men in a buggy. They hitch their hosses and come in the house, which scared me. Then one of the strangers said, Git your clothes, Mary. We has bought you from Mr. Shorter.' I commenced to cryin' an' beggin' Mr. Shorter not to let 'em take me away. But he said, 'Yes, Mary, I sold you and you must go with them.'

Then those strange men, whose names I ain't never knowed, took me an' put me in the buggy an' drive off with me, me hol-lerin' at the top of my voice an' callin' my ma. Then, them speculators [slave traders] begin to sing loud, just to drown out my hollerin'.

Us passed the very field where Paw an' all my folks was workin' an' I called out as loud as I could an' as long as I could see them, 'Goodbye, Ma! Goodbye, Ma!' But she never heard me. An' she couldn't see me, 'cause they had me pushed down out of sight on the floor of the buggy. I ain't never seed or heard tell of my Ma and Paw, an' brothers and sisters, from that day to this."

The Deepest Cut

There was a cruelty, however, that inflicted its pain far deeper than physical punishment ever could have, and yet only a few of its victims were even conscious of it. Those who were, such as the great orator and former slave Frederick Douglass, considered it even more damaging than the stinging whip or the shackles that turned black ankles red.

This particular cruelty affected the loyal and the disloyal, the well-treated and the oppressed, and the great mass of souls in-between. Because slaves were not free, none of them had been given the chance to become educated (academically, socially, or

Frederick Douglass, a former slave and noted orator, condemned slave owners for their failure to educate their slaves.

culturally), and, as a result, they appeared to lack the mental potentialities attributed to the ruling white race.

Most Southerners during the nineteenth century had never seen a black person read, write, speak proper English, or perform any tasks other than those simply requiring brute strength. It is understandable, when viewed from the perspective of that time, that whites considered blacks to be less capable than themselves.

The greater tragedy, however, lies in the similarly understandable fact that the slaves came to believe that same debilitating falsehood about themselves. And while dogs, chains, and slave catchers may have kept their bodies bound in servitude until their emancipation, the blacks' acceptance of their own inferiority kept them prisoners of white supremacy for many more years after that.

Notions of Superiority

It is important to note that this mistaken notion of black inferiority was not exclusive to the South. The overwhelming majority in the North subscribed to it as well. They had already experimented with and discarded slavery (for economic, more than moral reasons), but their contact with those "pitiable savages" had left them convinced that while blacks should not be enslaved, neither should they be integrated into Northern society on an equal basis. A panoply of prewar Northern segregation statutes attests to that.

In the South, it went without saying that the planter aristocracy regarded blacks as inferior. Many planters believed, with contemporary "scientific" justification, that slaves even belonged to a different species altogether. However, they also considered themselves superior to the white middle and

A Civil War–era photograph, taken on a Southern cotton plantation, shows a mammy and several children taking a stroll near the manor house.

lower classes as well, even when conceding that they were at least their racial equals.

What resulted between these three classes of whites was a tenuous and often uneasy bond that was partially strengthened by their shared prejudice against blacks and their fear of slave uprisings. During the early months of the Civil War, it appeared that those bonds would be further reinforced by the addition of yet another common threat: invading Yankees intent on loosing the angry, black hordes on them. It would remain to be seen whether the racial and cultural commonalities shared by the divergent classes of Southern whites would be enough to overcome the distrust that developed when they were all thrown together into the heated crucible of war. One thing was certain. If they did not band together for victory, they would surely be disbanded in utter defeat.

The Forgotten Majority

No group of Southern whites committed a greater portion of its resources to the crucible of war than the nonslave-holding middle class. These yeoman farmers, merchants, and craftsmen made up 80 percent of the Southern populace and 80 percent of the Confederate army's manpower while often losing 100 percent of all they held dear. Even knowing the possibility of such sacrifices, few men in the South proved any more willing to defend their way of life than these freedom-loving patriots, and over two hundred thousand of them died doing it. These citizen-warriors chose to make the protection of their homes and families their principal motivation for taking up arms. And with every mile closer to those homes that the invading army drew, the harder they fought to protect them.

Those Homes in Better Times

One popular type of dwelling place for the middle-class farmer in the South at the time of the Civil War was called the "saddlebag" house (or, sometimes, the "shotgun" house). It consisted of two usually identical self-contained squares or, as one observer noted, "two square pens with a large open space between them connected by an over-hanging roof above and a long porch and floor below."[67] Each square was divided into two rooms with lofts overhead for storage or

Soldiers tidy their winter quarters. Middle-class farmers, craftsmen, and merchants comprised 80 percent of the Confederate army. These hardworking soldiers made great sacrifices to defend their homes and families against the Federals.

A commonly accepted yet misleading assumption concerning the Civil War is that it was a war pitting "brother against brother." While there may have been some truth to that notion in border states such as Kentucky, West Virginia, Maryland, and Missouri, the bulk of the opposing soldiers hailed from widely divergent regions, bloodlines, and backgrounds.

A British woman traveling through America at the outset of the war observed:

> The South has become a separate people, dissevered from the North by habits, morals, institutions, pursuits, and every conceivable difference in their modes of thought and action. They have no bond but that of a meager political union. The South is seceding from the North because the two are not homogenous. They have different instincts, different appetites, different morals, and a different culture.

> Another said simply, "The South is culturally dominated by plain folk [the non-slave-holding middle class] whose ways are quite distinctive from those of Northerners." No, Yankees and Rebels were not brothers; they were barely even distant cousins. And, sadly, they were no better able to accept each other's differences than any two groups who ever went to war.

sleeping. The front room provided space for eating, indoor work, informal entertaining, cooking, and family gatherings around the hearth on firelit evenings.

A second room in the back (sometimes called the parlor or the chamber) was generally set aside as the parents' bedroom. It often doubled as a formal or ceremonial room, where the family's finest furniture, including the prized "big bed," would be proudly displayed for "proper company" to see.

The corresponding square across the breezeway offered living space and quarters for children, extended family members, hired hands, or even the slaves of the few middle-class families who owned one or two. Sometimes, a separate kitchen stood out back along with a barn, several sheds, and, of course, a privy.

A Look Inside

The rooms of the yeoman farmer's home blended the functional and the fashionable. The rough-timbered interior walls were often sheathed over with well-sanded boards and were, in some cases, even wallpapered. But papered or not, sheathed or not, the walls did a creditable job of keeping the winter cold within tolerable limits. Windows and the airy breezeway helped moderate the summer heat.

Even the larger rooms were, by no means, spacious, usually occupying no more than twenty-four by sixteen feet. One foreign traveler through the South mentioned seeing several middle-class houses that were even smaller than that. She said that the house of a Maryland family "looked as if three men might have overturned it, had they pushed hard against the gable end. It contained one room, about twelve feet square, and another adjoining it, hardly larger than a closet."[68] Such extreme dimensions can be misleading, however, because the kitchen, workers' quarters, and storage areas that many larger houses had on the inside were built apart from the smaller ones. But that notwithstanding, the rooms of the Southern yeomen's homes were, in most cases, inarguably small.

A Confederate family relaxes on the lawn of their home in 1862. Most middle-class homes were modestly furnished and included such items as the prized "big bed," elegant shelf clock, and modern curtains.

Making a House a Home

As small as the rooms may have been, they took on an air of respectability, even those that still had bare, wooden floors as opposed to carpets or rugs. Some enterprising house-wives painted blankets to make rugs or even painted ruglike patterns on the floor until they could afford the real items. The furniture, while not always of manufacturers' uniformity, revealed a skilled craftsman's hand. There might have been six or eight wooden kitchen chairs as well as a finished table large enough to accommodate them.

For those of more substantial means, one room might be furnished with "fancy chairs" (usually factory-made in the North) and a fancy table to match. Some homes even boasted an upholstered easy chair or a sofa, though they quickly lost popularity through-out most of the agricultural areas because their stuffing made such a comfortable home for rodents and lice.

Aside from the "big bed," a shelf clock did the most to establish a family's standing as being one of middle-class means. Children and adults alike would often gather around for the daily winding ritual and to stand in awe of its polished gold, shining mahogany, and mystifying machinations.

Window curtains also served as a status symbol. Since they had not been a common sight in the South prior to the 1850s, they became all the more sought after when machine-made textiles finally put them with-in reach of the middle-class budget. They quickly became an outward and visible sign of the family's upward mobility while afford-ing their owners a bit more privacy than unadorned windowpanes.

Lighting was a source of pride as well, especially if the family owned an astral lamp, a cut-glass oil lamp that cast a starlike glow. The highly refined sperm-whale oil they burned took on a reverence of its own, with its exotic origin, high price, and brighter light. They cost so much to operate, though, that most families still burned candles that they made themselves. Even the candles were used sparingly, though, for they burned down rapidly and were not easy to replace. So, often as not, the yeoman farmer and his family gathered around the hearth fire for light, singing songs, telling tales, and just listening to the fire crackle (a memory of family togetherness that most Southerners cherished for their entire lifetimes).

Children's Chores

The daily routine of the yeoman farmer and his family required grit, pluck, and plenty of hard work. A typical workday started at dawn when the father would arise in his long night-shirt and rap on the ceiling with a broomstick to awaken the children sleeping in the loft or those over in the other "saddlebag." The mother was usually already up by then fixing corn, salted pork, and corn pone over the hearth fire. As soon as the smaller children could be rousted and dressed, the parents sent them to gather eggs and milk the cow. The boys always opted to find the eggs (which might or might not be in the barn depending on how far the chickens had wandered during the night) since milking was considered woman's work. One boy remembered that it was "too 'gal-ish' for a boy to milk. My mother

Stage Advice

Poor roads and inclement weather made "highway" travel in the South exceedingly difficult, especially for those in the middle class. Wealthy people had their own comfortable carriages and personal drivers to minimize their discomfort while in transit, and the poor did not bother to travel at all. The majority in-between, however, had to crowd onto the public stagecoaches and follow the advice one newspaper offered, as quoted in McCutcheon's Everyday Life in the 1800s.

"The best seat inside a stagecoach is the one next to the driver. You will have to ride with your back to the horses, which with some people, produces an illness not unlike sea sickness, but on a long journey this will wear off, and you will get more rest, with less than half the bumps and jars than on any other seat. Bathe your feet before starting in cold weather, and wear loose overshoes and gloves two or three sizes too large. When the driver asks you to get off and walk, do it without grumbling. He will not request it unless absolutely necessary. If the team runs away, sit still and take your chances; if you jump, nine times out of ten you will be hurt.

Don't growl at food in stations; stage companies usually provide the best they can get. Don't keep the stage waiting. Don't smoke a strong pipe. Spit on the leeward side of the coach. If you have anything in a bottle, pass it around; a man who drinks by himself in such cases is lost to all human feeling. Don't swear. Don't lop over on your neighbor when sleeping. Don't ask how far it is to the next station. Never attempt to fire a gun or a pistol; it may frighten the team and make nervous people nervous. Don't grease your hair before starting or dust will stick there in sufficient quantities to make a respectable potato patch. Don't imagine for a moment you are going on a picnic; expect annoyance, discomfort, and hardships."

would have been mortified if any neighboring boy or man had caught me at it."[69]

After breakfast the younger boys and girls might undertake a task such as candle-dippin'. They would fill an outside kettle with pork or beef tallow (slimy, slippery fat) and cook it over an open fire until it melted. They then dangled several strings (wicks) from a piece of wood and dipped the strings repeatedly in the rancid-smelling tallow. The children let each preceding layer of "wax" dry before dipping the wicks again, thereby allowing the size of the candle to increase until, twenty-five to fifty dips later, they reached the desired size. They could make perhaps 120 candles in a morning.

Another job around the house in which children took part was the making of lye soap. Boys and girls shoveled the ashes out of the hearth and dripped water through them again and again. They caught the lye water each time it ran through and mixed it with tallow (that ever-useful fat). Older girls or the mother boiled down the stinking mixture until it thickened into a gray-white paste, at which time they spread it into pans, hardened it in the sun, and then cut it into highly abrasive cakes for laundering and bathing.

Girls also helped their mothers string slices of fruit together when it was in season to be dried and eaten during winter. Even

Soap making was an important job on Southern farms. After the ash and tallow mixture was thickened and spread into pans, the lye soap was left to harden in the sun until it could be cut into smaller cakes.

The chores performed by the industrious farm woman were never ending. In addition to teaching and caring for her children, she was responsible for all domestic tasks pertaining to the hearth, kitchen, house, garden, and farmyard.

more importantly, they assisted in the preserving and pickling of meats and vegetables to tide the family over during the cold, lean months. Many also provided an incalculable service to their families by learning how to gather and process plants for herbal medicines. Among others, they could pick yarrow for fever, pokeberry for arthritis, wild garlic (ramps) for colds, cherry bark for coughs, and coltsfoot for chest colds.

A Woman's Work Was Never Done

For all that the children did to help out, however, it was the women who performed most of the domestic labor. Their realm of responsibility embraced the hearth, kitchen, house, garden, and farmyard and included "the everyday work of the household." That included but was not limited to sewing, mending, cooking, serving, clearing away, washing dishes and clothing, and caring for

"half-a-score more or less of children" clamoring about their feet.[70]

Women also served as the primary teachers for those children, spending long hours before and after the workday, passing on what little learning they possessed. Since the few available schools were only open during the three winter months (and even then were usually too distant for most students to attend), mothers went over rote memorization lessons in an effort to teach their boys and girls how to read, write, and "cipher" well enough to study the Bible, correspond by letter, and manage money. As letters and diaries of the time attest, most never mastered spelling or grammar.

All other areas and applications of scholarship were considered superfluous to the requirements of farming . . . or soldiering, for that matter, as evidenced by one Union infantryman's remarks—when someone ridiculed the Southern fighting man's educational background in his presence, he replied, "They might not be able to read or

What's Your Sign?

Aside from the Bible, the most widely read printed matter during the mid-nineteenth century was the *Farmer's Almanac*. Farmers bought these paperback annuals in prodigious numbers not only for their funny stories and wise sayings, but also because they provided detailed weather predictions as they related to farming. While these predictions tended toward inaccuracy, farmers at the time were happy to take whatever help they could get when it came to divining droughts and early freezes. The weather reports, however, were only part of the almanacs' lure to the prudent farmers of the day. The trusted annuals also offered astrological information on which every aspect of the agricultural process could supposedly be based.

A rural Kentucky man recalled that

many things had to be done, or left undone, during the reign of each con-

stellation [that is, Gemini, Virgo, Aries, and so on]. The moon had a powerful influence on vegetation and animal life. Women planted radishes downward at the decrease of the moon, for they tapped downwards. Pork would shrink and wither away in the barrel [if it was slaughtered during the wrong astrological period].

Planet movements, comets, lunar eclipses, solar eclipses, constellation changes, the rising and setting times of the sun and moon, and tides were all predicted by almanacs with considerable accuracy. They further explained what the farmer should and should not do during each of these astrological occurrences, from planting to weaning calves to making butter. And even the most learned of agricultural scholars considered it as foolish to disregard the almanacs as to disregard the seasons themselves.

write too good but they sure as hell can shoot!"[71] And due to their mothers' Herculean efforts, most could read, write, and do arithmetic well enough to get along in the world. But teaching was barely a fraction of the work that women had to do.

From the dark of dawn to the dark of night, women husked corn, churned butter, pressed cheese, ground grain, and performed every conceivable chore requiring a spinning wheel, a loom, needles, soap, washtubs, baskets, cooking pots, and crockery. And more often than not, it was also the mothers around whom the children would gather for "doctorin'"—hugs and solace during all forms of suffering, physical and emotional, since the "younguns" were unlikely to get any of that from their fathers.

Lesser Lords but Lords Nonetheless

For hundreds of years in Europe and America, the men had ruled over the family, and they had done so with a stern and powerful hand. Their word was law, their decisions and decrees final. And whereas they loved their children as dearly as any parent could, they saw it as their responsibility to provide strict discipline and control over them, usually preferring to maintain a traditionally masculine air in their presence, which sometimes precluded open displays of affection.

They approached their work with much the same sense of masculinity, taking on every task requiring force, endurance, or the use of dangerous tools (and teaching the skills involved to their sons). Manhandling scythes, axes, plows, guns, knives, and saws, they plowed, planted, and harvested food crops, cotton, and tobacco; they mowed hay, hoed weeds, hunted, fished, cleared stony fields, pulled out stumps, felled trees, split rails, built fences, and hauled wood and water. Growing sons eventually took on some of these tasks (as growing daughters helped their mothers more at home), but the brunt of the heavy labor continued to fall upon the men's shoulders—at least until the war came.

The Women Take Over

The terrible casualties brought on by the Rebel "victories" of 1862 at such bloodbaths as Shiloh, the Peninsula, Second Manassas, Antietam, and Fredericksburg caused the Confederate government to begin conscripting men to replace the dead and wounded who had initially rushed off to "glory." Men between the ages of 18 and 35 (later 18 to 40 and then 17 to 50) who had been needed in their fields, stores, and craftsman shops for the first two years of the fighting were now drafted and marched off to war. That left their responsibilities in the hands of women, children, the aged, and the war-wounded, with the women typically assuming the leadership roles vacated by their husbands.

The task brought on many hardships, but women like Lucy Lowe met them with pluck. In a letter to her husband, she wrote:

John,
    Your corn is out now and I have not drawed anything yet. Pane (the hired hand) has quit and left the crop in a bad fix. I have got the rye cut and sent to market. Your old mare is gone blind in one eye and something is the matter with one of her feet. Your hogs and cows is coming along very well. I want you to come home for I want to see you so bad I don't know what to do. I remain your loving wife until death.

    Goodbye to you, Lucy.[72]

As hordes of Southern men left their homes to join the army, their normal farm duties were relegated to the women and children they left behind. Southern women still performed their domestic duties, including candle making (pictured), but they also had to tend to the crops and take care of financial matters.

Growling Stomachs and Frazzled Nerves

Food shortages of all kinds began adding to the home folks' misery in 1862. Coffee supplies dwindled first. The Union naval blockade was tightening its stranglehold on Southern ports, cutting off such imported "luxury items." The Southerners improvised as best they could with coffee substitutes made from sweet potatoes, peanuts, rye, corn, or okra, but only the most patriotic among them would claim that any of these really tasted like coffee or stimulated them the way that real coffee did. Some tried to kick the coffee habit altogether and turned to berry and sassafras tea, but few found any of it very satisfying.

Access to sugar similarly waned as the Federals cut off rail and river traffic within the South (except in southern Louisiana and Mississippi, where sugarcane grew). Confederate civilians compensated with sorghum molasses, honey, and watermelon syrup, so pies, cakes, and candies continued to sweeten meals but in not quite as delicious a way. Beef and dairy cattle, pigs, and chickens disappeared any time soldiers from either army passed nearby, causing many farm women to feed their children with salted or pickled pork, if they had possessed the foresight to can and store it up during better times.

Subjected to these privations, Amie Kelley wrote her husband:

> My Dearest S.,
> Brother James has sold your corn but there was only 60¼ bushels. You say I must sell a mule if I am out of money but

Houses stand in ruins in war-torn Fredericksburg after the Rebels ripped through the city. The Confederates incurred extremely high numbers of casualties during their bloody campaigns of 1862, causing them to begin conscripting men who had previously been needed on the homefront.

A Southern woman and her children harvest wheat in this 1863 woodcut. Without men to help with the laborious task of planting and harvesting crops, many Southern cities faced famine as the overworked women tried to manage their homes and their farms without the funds necessary to efficiently run both.

I will wait. We are needing rain. The weather is dry and hot and I feel like it is for our sins that these things come upon us. Truly these are trying times and who will be able to stand. Brother Smith was here day before yesterday. He looks badly and limps a little. He says we did not near whip the Yanks at Richmond. They are reinforcing for another fight. Be a good soldier and maybe it will not be long till we can sit at home together.

Goodbye, Amie.[73]

"I Am So Tired"

The absence of men compounded the food shortages in spite of the heroic attempts by women to compensate for their being gone.

The spring plantings and fall harvests in particular required skills, strengths, and time that most women simply did not have. And since farmers small and large had to cut back on cash crops like cotton and tobacco in order to grow enough food to survive, the women had no cash crop money with which to hire any available laborers.

Just as vexing, farm equipment kept on breaking down from ordinary wear and tear, and few replacement parts could be found. Most agricultural machines had been purchased from Northern factories before the war, and the Southern machine shops capable of repairing them had been converted to making war matériel.

Salt shortages proved to be among the most damaging, however, for without it meat could not be preserved. That meant that if a family could somehow manage to obtain a cow or a pig, they would end up having to throw out all the meat except that which they could eat in the day or two before it spoiled.

While her husband fought the Yankees in Virginia, Mary Frances Brooks endured all of these problems and still kept the farm running, cared for their four children, and gave them an education. The pressure of those responsibilities and the loneliness caused by being separated from her beloved partner throb in each of her poignant lines:

> This letter leaves me and the family well but I am so tired for I never get any rest night or day, and I don't think I will last much longer, but I will write to you as long as you stay there, if I can raise a pen. The children are getting along tolerable well. They all want to see you and talk of you very often. Money is getting low with me. I have got to buy bacon, and haven't any salt, and no one to see to it without pay. I want you home in the worst sort of way.
>
> Farewell, Mary.[74]

"There Is No Pity Here"

Perhaps the most pernicious of all reasons for the privations and hardships came from the Southerners themselves or at least one despicable group among them. They were the speculators who bought up and hoarded hard-to-find dry goods and foods and refused to sell them until prices went up (which inevitably happened because of their hoarding!). This nefarious practice added to the inflation necessarily resulting from the war and was felt by everyone on the home front.

One seventy-two-year-old Georgia widow petitioned her governor in hopes of getting her only supporting son released from the army. She needed the young man to help earn enough money to pay a fifty-dollar debt, the nonpayment of which would result in the forfeiture of her farm. "I fear the speculators will prove too hard for us," she wrote, "as they have everything and I have so little to buy it with. Sometimes I am almost ready to give up the struggle as there is no pity here."[75]

And as bad as things were, they were about to get worse.

6

Mountaineers, "Crackers," and Other "Traitors"

The year 1863 introduced the beginning of the end for the Confederacy. After suffering major military losses at Gettysburg, Pennsylvania; Vicksburg, Mississippi; and Chattanooga, Tennessee, the Rebel armies were retreating on all fronts. At home, food, firewood, clothing, and transportation became next to impossible to obtain. However, the very poorest Southerners in the mountains, swamps, and pine barrens grappled on with survival the way they had always done, barely noticing any changes brought on by the war.

Mountaineers: Wretched and Free

One Rebel private tramping through the northern Alabama mountains wrote of their coarse ways, "The state of the morals is quite as low as the soil, almost all the women look as if they would be given to whoredom and are the ugliest, most sallow-faced, shaggy headed, bare-footed dirty wretches you ever saw."[76] But these grimy-faced mountaineers could not have cared less what anyone

Life for Southern mountaineers remained relatively unchanged during the Civil War. Living in remote areas with only the barest of necessities, these poor Southerners were isolated from the bloody battles and supply shortages taking place in the cities.

thought of them because they depended upon no one but themselves for sustenance. What they needed, they made or made due without, be that food, clothing, or shelter. Long before freedom and independence had become fashionable watchwords among soldiers and secessionists, these hill dwellers lived wild and unfettered. They relied on their wits, surviving or perishing as a result of no other efforts but their own.

Just eight years after the Civil War, a Northern reporter by the name of Edward King traveled throughout the recently defeated South and described the mountaineers he met:

> The tall, lean, sickly farmer, clad in a homespun pair of trousers and a flax shirt, with the omnipresent gray slouched hat drawn down over his forehead, courteously greeted us. Buttermilk and biscuits were served; we conversed with the farmer on his condition.

> He cultivated a small farm, like most of the neighbors in moderate circum-

In the Paths of Angry Armies

Civilians in the piney woods and mountain areas of the South suffered doubly during the Civil War. Those suspected of being Union supporters were singled out for abuse by bands of Confederate scouts, renegades, and desperadoes, while Federal soldiers took particular pleasure in terrorizing the "country bumpkins." The double-edged problem for all backland civilians was that neither army could ever be fully convinced as to a person's loyalty, so all soldiers, North and South, played it safe and took advantage of everyone in their paths.

Some well-intentioned Union officers would post guards to defend the property of Southerners but often failed to insure that they performed their job well. One Yankee private remarked:

> Our soldiers don't make very good guards in such cases. I know of some who couldn't see a Union soldier picking peaches in the orchard they were set to guard and others were kind enough to point out the best trees and turn their backs.

The draft of a Federal court-martial revealed a more serious abuse of power:

> A party entered the dwelling of Milly Ann Clayton and opened all the trunks, drawers, and boxes of every description, and taking out the contents thereof destroyed, spoiled, or carried away the same. They also insulted the said Milly Ann Clayton and threatened to shoot her, and then proceeding to the kitchen, they there attempted an indecent outrage on her person.

It is not clear whether these offenders were punished or not or even whether court-martials in general did anything to reduce such crimes against Southern civilians. What is very clear, though, is that home folk in the paths of advancing armies found themselves at the mercy of armed, angry, and often brutality-hardened men who had suffered enough as soldiers to care very little about the suffering of civilians.

The barren interior of a mountaineer's home. These Southern hill dwellers lived primitively but were self-sufficient, growing or making whatever their families needed to survive.

stances; he only grew corn enough for his own support. There was very little money in all the region round about; farmers rarely saw fifty dollars in cash from year to year; the few things they needed from the outside they got by barter. He said his ten children were usually responsible for minding the pigs around the cabin, and caring for the stock. The girls and boys work afield with their parents in the summer, and pass the winter with but limited chances for culture.

The housewife was smoking her corn-cob pipe, and sitting rather disconsolately before the fireplace, warming her thin hands by the few remaining coals in the ashes. The rain dripped in through the roof and the children were huddled mutely together where it could not reach them. The furnishings were, as everywhere among the poorer classes in the mountains, of the plainest character. But

the log barn was amply provisioned; stock looked well, and a few sheep and goats were amicably grouped under the shed.[77]

Loyalties, Apathies, and Ancient Grudges

Prior to observing these mountaineers, King toured the swamps and pine barrens of southern Georgia, where he encountered another subgroup of Southerners who had been equally cut off from the war and civilization. King reflected the commonly held view among whites when he wrote:

In the lower part of the State, in the piney woods and swamps, the inhabitants are indolent, uneducated, complaining and shiftless. Their indolence, ignorance, and remoteness from any well-ordered farming regions are the excuses. These are the sallow and lean people who always feel

Hogs race out of harm's way as soldiers forage for their dinner on a poor Southern farm. The impressment tax allowed soldiers to take food, clothing, and any other needed supplies from the already strained Southern citizens.

"tolerable" but who never feel well; a people of dry fibre and coarse existence, yet devoid of wit and good sense.

The Georgia "cracker" is eminently shiftless; he seems to fancy that he was born with his hands in his pockets, his back curved, and his slouch hat crowed over his eyes, and does his best to maintain this attitude forever. His quarrels grow into feuds, cherished for many years, until some day, at a cross-roads or a country tavern, a pistol or a knife puts a bloody and often fatal end to the difficulty.[78]

One poor white who refused to serve in the Rebel army spoke for many when he said simply, "Then as wants to fight, let 'em fight. I don't!"[79] And who could have blamed them? Planters and the middle class had long treated them as inferiors who ranked beneath even the slaves in value, driving them to either profess an outward loyalty to the Union or to ignore the war altogether.

Revenuers: An Old Enemy with New Tricks

By the spring of 1863, the Confederate government was running out of money with which to pay for the war. Times of crisis often call for novel solutions, and the economic wizards in Richmond went to work on devis-

A Southern Hero's Dissent

Mountaineers, "crackers," and starving city dwellers were not the only people who found some reason to oppose secession. Government leaders, military men, and Southern idols of all types spoke out against it before and during the war.

Sam Houston fought for Texas's independence from Mexico (at the time of the Alamo), served as president of the Republic of Texas that resulted and as U.S. senator and governor of the state of Texas after it was admitted to the Union. When the question of secession arose, however, he parted ways with those who had followed him so devotedly, warning:

> Let me tell you what is coming. Your fathers and husbands, your sons and brothers, will be herded at the point of the bayonet. You may, after the sacrifice of countless millions of treasure and hundreds of thousands of lives, as a bare possibility, win Southern independence. But I doubt it. I believe with you in the doctrine of States' Rights but the North is determined to preserve this Union.

Texas seceded anyway and the once-adoring Texans removed Houston from the governorship.

It is interesting to note that many who disapproved of this "defeatist" when their bellies were full and their roofs were securely over their heads came to agree with him as more and more of his predictions came to pass.

ing their own. What they came up with were three means of taxation, none of which had ever been tried before: an income tax, an impressment tax, and a tax in kind.

The income tax, a 10 percent levy on salaries, raised more money from the middle class than the lower classes because many of them held jobs that generated taxable paychecks. Impoverished whites rarely worked for a regular salary and so felt few effects from the tax. Impressment and the tax in kind, however, proved more intrusive to the poor farmers. Impressment allowed the army to seize goods such as food, clothing, horses, wagons, and livestock as needed, while the tax in kind permitted revenue officials to demand 10 percent of those items on a regular, preestablished schedule.

Even among the middle and upper classes, an outcry erupted every time "revenuers" or army foragers came around. One anecdote floating around among them "joked" that "the Yankees could do us no more harm than our own soldiers have."[80] But most planters and yeomen at least believed in the causes of the struggle and knew that the taxes were necessary evils. The same could not be said for the mountaineers and swampers, though, and by midwar they had discovered a new way in which to stymie the Confederate taxmen.

Aiding and Abetting

The disappointments and disasters suffered by the soldiers of the Confederacy through 1863 drove nearly two hundred thousand brave and otherwise dedicated men to go absent without leave. Letters from home such as the following render their dereliction of duty understandable:

Some two hundred thousand soldiers deserted the Confederate army, many of them heading south to rescue their own families from the ravishes of war.

However, one-fifth of a million men going AWOL (absent without leave) was extremely notable to the Confederate army, and all of those deserters knew it. Many believed they would be apprehended and shot if they remained at home for long, so after doing what they could for their families, thousands escaped into the mountains, swamps, and pine barrens. The well-armed renegades banded together into groups of twenty-five or fifty or even a hundred and vowed not to be taken alive. They formed pacts with the natives, offering them help around their farms and protection from tax collectors in exchange for food, clothing, and warnings of approaching Confederate officials. They knew that Southern soldiers would come looking for them. And they wasted no time in preparing ambushes for their former comrades.

> Our son is lying at death's door. He cannot live long for the fix he is in. He is raving distracted. His earnest calls for his Pa almost break my heart. John, come if you can. If they will not let you off, I don't know the reason.[81]

Another desperate wife wrote:

> We haven't got nothing in the house to eat but a bit of meal. Try to get off and come home and fix us all up some and then you can go back. If you put off coming, t'won't be no use to come, for we'll all be out there in the garden in the graveyard with your ma and mine.[82]

Considering such poignant pleas, it seems less notable that two hundred thousand soldiers fled the Rebel armies than the fact that a million men bravely remained at their posts.

A Civil War Within a Civil War

The killing began gradually and in small numbers. An officer in Georgia and two in North Carolina were ambushed and murdered as they made their way into the mountains to round up deserters. Elsewhere in North Carolina, other "officers were sometimes shot by deserters and communities [loyal to the South] kept in terror."[83]

As the numbers of deserters increased, the size of their territories grew until some gangs boasted control over entire counties, swamps, and mountains. One clan reigned over a mountainous county in southwestern Virginia and attracted desperate men from all over Virginia, West Virginia, Kentucky, and Tennessee; another took over twenty-five hundred square miles of the South Carolina hills and claimed responsibility for several dead bodies that turned up there. A Rebel officer who had escaped from those hills with his life wrote, "The people there are poor, ill-informed, and but little identified with our struggle. They have been easily seduced from their duty."[84]

Perhaps the best known and most feared of the deserter fiefdoms existed in Jones County, Mississippi, and, hence, took the name the Republic of Jones. A shoemaker by the name of Newton Knight organized a Union guerrilla band based out of the hills, forests, and marshes there and expanded his activities from small ambushes designed to murder one or two tax collectors to full-scale raids on Confederate columns. So many corpses began to appear around the "republic" that one local citizen remarked, "If a man is found dead, the civil authorities pays no attention to it—any more than if it was a dog."[85] The bushwhackers created a safe haven for deserters and security for the Unionist citizens who lived in those backwoods. They stymied Rebel operations in the area until the end of the war, and their "republic" never fell.

Revenge and Beyond

Not all guerrillas were as fortunate as those in the Republic of Jones. Fifty North Carolina deserters who had terrorized a snowbound village in search of salt and booty made the mistake of ransacking their former colonel's home, hastening the deaths of his two sick children. That colonel, one Lawrence Allen, tracked his former soldiers back up into the wintry mountains and swiftly took revenge. After killing thirty of the offenders in running gun battles, Allen turned his fury on the mountaineers, who he believed were protecting the rest.

He tortured and whipped women, children, and old men until they divulged the hiding places of another fifteen deserters.

Supplied with that information, Colonel Allen and his men surprised this final group and took them prisoner, whereupon the colonel remembered his commanding general's parting words, "I do not want to be troubled with prisoners. . . . The last one of them should be killed."[86] Allen then commanded the cold-blooded execution of each of them with a single bullet through the brain. He then left their bodies in the bloody snow for a herd of hungry hogs to devour.

The Cities Simmer

The mountains and the swamps were not the only breeding grounds of rancor between Southerners. Several cities were also rife with dissent, although it was due more to hunger than ideology or revenge. A significant source of unrest in the cities was the press, in particular those newspapers writing articles critical of the Confederate war effort. General Robert E. Lee expressed his frustration with this reporting, reflecting on the nature of the editors: "These men seem to prefer sowing discord to inculcating harmony."[87] And they did it well. By 1863 provocative editorials had stirred up the citizens' passions over the growing shortages of food and agitated them into taking matters into their own hands.

Journalists enflamed civilians with articles (usually truthful ones) about how the astronomical inflation was being caused by the government's printing of too much paper money. As with anything else, they wrote, the more there was of it, the less value it had and, hence, the diminished buying power. A Virginia man wrote sarcastically:

Money was never so plentiful—Confederate States Treasury Notes, Bank Notes of all sorts and sizes, and "shinplasters"

The Pitied and the Scorned

The refugees flooding into the cities from the Yankee-controlled countryside exacerbated the starvation already prevalent there. But even before reaching the urban blight, the hardships of the displaced Southerners were well under way. They were homeless, foodless, penniless, and vulnerable to every thief, disease, and danger of the open road. Having piled their wagons high with all their earthly belongings, they endured days and weeks on the roads to the cities, mistakenly thinking they would be welcome there.

The refugees offered a pathetic sight to one woman who watched them pass. She said:

They were hatless, bonnetless, some with slippers and no stockings, some with wrappers hastily thrown over nightgowns. Now and then a coatless man on a bare-back horse holding a helpless child in his arms, and a terrified woman clinging on behind. There were about five hundred tired, exhausted, broken-down, sick, frightened, terrified human beings.

The refugees themselves quickly discovered that shortages existed everywhere and that they were not welcome to share the few supplies to which the local residents had access. One homeless woman wrote:

The more we see of people, the less we like them, and every refugee we have seen feels the same way. The local people call us renegades. It is strange the prejudice that exists all through the state against refugees.

And yet another reason for dissent and dissatisfaction wrapped its tentacles around the dying Confederacy.

Southerners flee their homes as the Union army approaches. These penniless refugees often traveled to neighboring cities in hopes of finding shelter and food but were often turned away by the local residents.

issued by towns, corporations and Tom, Dick, and Harry. Gold and silver are never seen.[88]

After three years of war, it took $3,400 to purchase what had originally been $120 worth of goods (and few could come up with the $3,400). Flour skyrocketed from $200 to $1,100 a barrel, cornmeal went from $20 to $100 a bushel, and bacon soared from $2 to $20 a pound. "You take your money to market in a basket," a joke went, "and bring home what you buy in your pocketbook."[89]

A heavy-laden Georgia mechanic wrote in 1863:

I once got 25 pounds of bacon for a day's work. What do I get now? Only two. I once got fifty pounds of beef for a day's work. What do I get now? Only six. I could once get 8 bushels of sweet potatoes for a day's work. What can I get now? Not one.[90]

One of the great tragedies of the Southern food shortage was that in some rural areas, there was an actual surplus of farm produce. It often rotted, though, before it could be transported to the cities because the railroads and waterways had been captured or damaged by the advancing Yankees. An exasperated Confederate War Department clerk felt driven to complain against his government concerning the results of all this on his family. "We are in a half-starving condition," he said. "I have lost twenty pounds and my wife and children are emaciated to some extent."[91]

Causing even more harm, government-condoned speculators continued to buy up and hold on to much of the available food, waiting for prices to rise even higher before selling it to the rich for huge profits. And as the common people grew hungrier and increasingly desperate, speculators and the store owners they supplied finally pushed them to the flash point of action.

The Bread Riot

On April 2, 1863, a tall "Amazon-looking woman" by the name of Mary Jackson waved a six-shooting revolver over her head and rallied a group of starving Richmond women to action. She implored them in a mighty voice to rise up and march with her to demand an audience with the governor to assert their basic right to eat. With fierce dark eyes and a firmly set brow, she led the mob through the muddy streets and beckoned both men and women along the way to join in. The agitated horde reached the capitol, numbering well into the hundreds, and Jackson orchestrated their vociferous demands into roars.

After several loud, angry minutes of crying out for fair food prices, the governor appeared and they quieted to give him a chance to speak. But they did not hear him say that he would offer them any relief so they booed him down and retook to the streets. Numbering well over a thousand by then, the raucous throng invaded the shop district and exploded into a riot. They broke windows, brandished knives, fired off pistols, and poured into stores, taking clothing, valuables, and, most of all, food.

Uncompromising Jefferson Davis

Nearly an hour of full-scale pandemonium ensued, filled with wild screams, chaotic laughter, and desperate fighting among the rioters over who would steal what. Finally, a hundred Confederate soldiers lined up at one

On April 2, 1863, pandemonium broke out in the streets of Richmond as angry mobs demanded that the government relieve their starvation. When Richmond's governor failed to satisfy the raucous Southerners, the mob began rioting and looting in the shop district.

end of the main street and, with fixed bayonets, began to slowly prod the crush of dissenters back toward the capitol. President Jefferson Davis himself met them this time, standing tall in the back of a wagon. The rioters treated him with no more respect than they had the governor, and they surged around the wagon with ravenous eyes and shaking fists.

Appearing nervous yet resolute, Davis cried over the boos, "you say you are hungry and have no money—here is all I have. It is not much but take it!" And he tossed out several coins that drove those nearest to them into a frenzy. The rest, however, pressed closer and shouted him down more vehemently.

He raised his voice higher, saying: "The Yankees are the authors of all our troubles,

not the government! Blame them!" When reason had no effect, however, he pulled out his pocket watch and announced, "We do not wish to injure anyone, but this lawlessness must stop. I will give you five minutes to disperse. Otherwise you will be fired upon." [92]

The mob hushed, but no one budged. The soldiers rattled their rifles to the ready. After an aching four-minute silence, Presi-

Confederate president Jefferson Davis stood firm against the demands of the rowdy mob during the Richmond Bread Riot. Davis advised the angry rioters to blame the Yankees for their food shortages, not his Confederacy.

"Seames as Every Body Was Happie"

The following account from The Foxfire Book *of a woman's childhood describes events that transpired around the turn of the century and yet reveals the same spirit of individualism and self-reliance that defined mountaineers before and during the Civil War.*

"my dadie raised the stuff we lived on   he groed the corn to make our bread   he groed the cane to make our syrup allso groed the beans and peas to make the soup beans out of and dried leather britches beans and dried fruit enough to last all winter   he killed enough meat to last all winter

he killed a beaf and a sheep and two or three hogs for the winter   he diden have mutch money for anything   my dad usto make our shoes   my mother usto weave wool cloth to make blankets and clothes out of   I have worn wool dresses   my mother allso knit our stockings and socks   I have help my dad shear sheep to get that wool   my mother would wash it and spin it into thread and then weave it on her loom

I usto help my brothers saw wood to make fires out of to keep warm   it was pretty hard to keep warm by an open fire but we was never sick back then   we played out the bigest snow ever come   we has a spring to carry watter from and my dad had to take his shovel and ditch out a way through the snow for us to get to the spring   the snow was waist deep

seames as every body was happie   we usto make our play houses out in the woods make our rag dolls to play with   my brothers sawed pine wagon wheels and made wagons to play with   one Christmas Santa Clause gave us three of four sticks of candie and a orange   he put it in our stocking and was as pleased as if he had given us a box full of candy"

---

dent Davis studied his watch and firmed his tone, "My friends, you have one minute left." Surely he would not fire on women, everyone wanted to think. But they knew of the uncompromising man's reputation for not backing down, and as the final sweaty seconds ticked off, the crowd began to break up, a few at a time and then the entire mass. And certainly no one must have felt any greater relief than Jefferson Davis himself.

So ended the Richmond Bread Riot but not the underlying causes for it. The same shortages and high prices touched off similar urban disturbances in Georgia, Tennessee, North Carolina, and Alabama. Though the rioting women in all of these outbursts were put down (and their leaders often jailed), they had at least made their point known and confirmed what a newspaper editor had earlier written: "If we are defeated, it will be by the people at home."[93] And with fresh legions of Federal troops poised to invade the heartland, no one expected the dissatisfaction of the people at home to ease.

Total War/Utter Destruction

Shortages, conscription, evacuations, robberies, riots, bushwhackings, and imprisonment all traumatized Southerners during the first two years of the war. Homes were burned, valuables stolen; citizens suffered beatings, executions, and forced relocations. Very little of that, however, was actually due to combat. Before 1863 most Southern people, black and white, had not yet directly suffered the horrors of battle. That would all change, though, in a prosperous little town overlooking the Mississippi River called Vicksburg.

Trapped Like the Rats They Ate

One of the last Southern-held towns that could block Federal traffic on the Mississippi River was Vicksburg, Mississippi. The troops and artillery emplaced on the high bluffs there could rain down fire and brimstone on any Union vessel attempting to pass below them. Several direct Union attacks against the fortress city had failed, causing the Federals to resort to siege warfare. The citizens of Vicksburg watched helplessly as the Yankees surrounded their town and began to bombard them.

One of them remembered the first shelling:

> Loud explosions shook the city to its foundations; shot and shell went hissing through the trees and walls, scattering fragments far and wide in their terrific flight; men, women, and children rushed into the streets, and amid the crash of

Citizens of Vicksburg, Mississippi, were forced to take refuge in caves as the Federals surrounded and bombarded their city.

Union and Confederate forces face off during the siege of Vicksburg. During this important battle, Federal officials declared Southern civilians to be legitimate military targets. As a result, nearly one dozen civilians were killed and another three dozen were wounded.

falling houses commenced hasty flight to their caves for shelter.[94]

Excerpts from a woman's diary particularly illuminated the hardships of trying to survive in such caves.

The cave gives me an earthy, suffocating feeling, as if living in a tomb. It is dreadful to me. I never understood before the full force of the questions: what shall we eat, what shall we drink, how shall we be clothed? We are utterly cut off from the world, surrounded by a circle of fire. The fiery shower of shells goes on day and night. Clothing cannot be washed or anything else. I pay five dollars a day for a small piece of mule meat. The cats and dogs have all disappeared, presumably eaten. Rats are being dressed and sold as food. We are dipping water from ditches and mudholes.[95]

After six blazingly hot weeks, the Confederates finally surrendered Vicksburg. And while civilian casualties were surprisingly low (approximately one dozen killed and another three dozen wounded), they had a profound effect on all Southerners remaining in the Yankees' paths. For the civilian dead and wounded symbolized a history-making change in the aims of the federal war machine. At last, the leadership in Washington had officially designated the Southern civilians as legitimate military targets deserving of dislocation or death if they offered any resistance whatsoever to the Union onslaught.

A photograph taken on July 25, 1864, shows one of the powerful siege guns at Petersburg, Virginia. The Union's bombardment of the important railroad center lasted an excruciatingly long ten months.

Petersburg: Key to the Capital

By 1864 that onslaught had advanced the Yankees to Petersburg, Virginia, a railroad center critical to the survival of Richmond. Unable to take this entrenched bastion by frontal assault, the Federals dug their own trenches and settled in for what would become a long siege. Petersburg itself stood a scant few miles from the front, and numerous batteries of mammoth Union siege guns could reach it at will. Morning and evening the Yankees turned those big guns on the city, eventually destroying or damaging some eight hundred buildings.

Refugees and the bombed-out homeless set up makeshift tents in backyards and parks and sought shelter in cellars when the shells screamed down. As in Vicksburg, relatively few civilians lost their lives (some reports listed as few as six), but, unlike Vicksburg, the bombardment continued for ten full months, not just a month and a half, and it created not only the obvious dangers of high explosives and shrapnel but critical shortages of food as well.

Civilians and soldiers, enduring the same privations, were increasingly seen to "pant and grow faint." One man said, "I thanked God I had a backbone for my stomach to lean up against." The little bacon that could be found had

> a peculiarly scaly color, spotted like a half-well case of smallpox, full of rancid odor, and utterly devoid of grease. It imparted a stinking odor when boiled. You could put a piece in your mouth and chew it for a long time, and the longer you chewed it the bigger it got. Then, by a desperate effort, you would gulp it down. Out of sight, out of mind.[96]

Another man wrote:

> Our living now is very poor, nothing but cornbread and poor beef, blue and

Free at Last . . . Or Were They?

Ironically, the first people to be dislocated by the war were the blacks, many of whom flocked to the Union army whenever they came into view. The Federals failed to convince the slaves that they had not come down South to take care of them, and after a while they began feeding and sheltering them anyway. Following a raid near Vicksburg, Union general William T. Sherman reported wryly, "We bring in some five hundred prisoners, a good many refugees, and about ten miles of Negroes." The sight of so many dispossessed blacks burdening the resources of the camps prompted one Union soldier to say, "I don't think enough of the nigger no more to go and fight for them."

The great numbers of runaway slaves could not have cared less, though. They were jubilant to be free, at least initially. The realities of homelessness, however, sobered most of them up rather quickly. A slave by the name of Jake Goodridge recalled:

The Yankee soldiers give out news of Freedom. They was shouting around. I just stood around to see what they was gonna do next. Didn't nobody give me nothin'. I didn't know what to do next. Everything's gone. Tents all gone, no place to stay and nothin' to eat. That was the big freedom to us colored folks. I got hungry and naked and cold many a time. I had a good master and I thought he always treated me a heap better than that. I wanted to go back, but I had no way.

Newly freed blacks find food and shelter in a freedmen's camp outside of Richmond in June 1865.

tough; no vegetables, no coffee, sugar, tea, or even molasses. I merely eat to live. You would laugh or cry to see me eating my supper, a pone of corn-bread and a tin cup of water. We have meat only once a week. It is hard to maintain one's patriotism on ashcake and water.[97]

Nevertheless, Southern patriotism would hold out in Petersburg until the very last weeks of the war, creating at least a glimmer of hope in nearby Richmond that some miracle of salvation might yet occur. Such a miracle would not be forthcoming, however, and Richmond would fall in a frenetic display of panic and fire; but not before the citizenry of Virginia's Shenandoah Valley first succumbed to the vengeful torches of the Union army.

Burning the Breadbasket

The great expanse of fertile flatland between the Blue Ridge and the Allegheny Mountains had long been the primary source of crops for both the Confederate army and the citizens of the upper South. Running north and south from Winchester to Roanoke, it also made for an excellent invasion route for the Confederates heading north and, toward the end of the war, for the Federals invading the South.

Union general Ulysses S. Grant wanted to strip this bountiful valley of anything that might aid or assist the Confederates, so he issued a stark and unyielding order to be carried out directly against the Southern farmers and townsfolk living there. "Leave nothing," he commanded, "to invite the enemy to return. Destroy whatever cannot be consumed. Let that valley be so left that crows flying over it will have to carry their own rations along with them."[98]

And that is nearly what happened. Under the despised General David Hunter and, later, General Philip Sheridan, Union troops went to war against anything Southern in the valley. They defeated the small Confederate army stationed there, leaving

A young Confederate soldier lies dead in a trench after the Battle of Petersburg.

A Southern woman recounts to Confederate soldiers the tale of her escape from the Shenandoah Valley. After the Yankees defeated the small company of Rebels stationed in the valley, the desperate citizens were forced to flee their homes or face death.

the unprotected civilians only three options: death, injury, or flight. Hampered only by Rebel partisan guerrillas, the Federals carried out General Grant's orders with ruthless efficiency, driving hordes to the roads as penniless refugees.

A Confederate officer reported that they "burnt mills, furnaces, storehouses, granaries, and all farming utensils they could find, beside a great amount of fencing, and a large quantity of grain. In Lexington, they burnt the Virginia Military Institute, and all the professors' houses."[99]

A young Southern diarist described the typical treatment of occupied homes, writing that her friend's house

had been sacked and everything carried off—every particle of grain, meat, or food in every possible shape, inanimate

or living. 15 horses, furniture, clothing, bedding, silver—in fact all she owned in the world except her wedding ring. The house was not only completely stripped but the walls ripped open and even the privies searched for hidden articles.[100]

Only in Georgia and South Carolina would the treatment be any worse.

Atlanta: Shelled, Evacuated, and Burned

While the Yankees were devastating the Shenandoah Valley, Union general William T. Sherman was doing the same thing to northern Georgia. He had encountered considerably more military resistance on the road to

After evacuating and burning Atlanta, Union general William T. Sherman continued to torment Southerners during his 275-mile march to the sea.

ments of the distress that will be occasioned by the evacuation, and yet shall not revoke my orders, simply because my orders are not designed to meet the humanities of the case.[103]

Indeed, after the battered city fell, General Sherman drove miles of top-heavy wagons, emaciated mules and horses, and barefooted, straggling families onto the roads south. He punctuated the desolation by burning a great portion of the city to the ground. Then, further ignoring the humanities of the case, Sherman started his army toward Savannah in a sixty-mile-wide swath, declaring, "I can make this march, and make Georgia howl![104]

The March to the Sea

Sherman gloated:

> Behind us lay Atlanta, smouldering and in ruins, the black smoke rising high in the air and hanging like a pall. . . . I now propose to demonstrate the vulnerability of the rest of the South and make its inhabitants feel that war and individual ruin are synonymous terms.[105]

Those terms suited the ravenous Yankee soldiers just fine. Covering 15 miles per day (of which would eventually be a 275-mile journey), they foraged, commandeered, cleaned out, trespassed, overran, offended, shot, bayoneted, slaughtered, and swooped down upon every conceivable property or belonging on every farm, town, and village between themselves and the Atlantic Ocean.

One Southern widow remembered,

> Like demons they rushed in! My yards were full. To my smoke-house, my dairy,

Atlanta than his counterparts had in Virginia, but he and his outnumbering legions eventually surrounded the fortified city and vowed to "make the inside of Atlanta too hot to be endured."[101] Justifying his siege of civilians, Sherman said, "War is cruelty. There is no use trying to reform it. The crueler it is, the sooner it will be over."[102]

When the Confederate commander appealed to him to stop bombarding the citizens of Atlanta, Sherman announced his intended plans to not only continue the shelling but to evacuate and make homeless the city's survivors once they surrendered.

> I have deemed it to the interest of the United States that the citizens now residing in Atlanta should be removed, those who prefer it to go South and the rest North. I give full credit to your state-

pantry, kitchen, and cellar, like famished wolves they came, breaking locks and whatever was in their way. The meat in my smoke-house was gone in a twinkling, my flour, my meat, my lard, butter, eggs, pickles both in vinegar and brine, wine, jars, and jugs were all gone. My fat turkeys, my hens, chickens and fowl, my young pigs, were all shot down in my yard and hunted as if they were the Rebels themselves.[106]

Sherman's soldiers burned down homes, farm buildings, and businesses and otherwise destroyed railroads, telegraphs, boats, roads, and bridges. As far as the Yankees were concerned, if an object had a purpose, it could serve the South, so they somehow managed to obliterate it.

A young Georgia girl described Sherman's "burnt country" this way:

The fields were trampled down and the road was lined with carcasses of horses, hogs, and cattle that the invaders had wantonly shot down to starve people out. The stench was unbearable. On every plantation we saw charred remains. Lone chimney stacks, "Sherman's sentinels," told of homes laid in ashes. The poor people were wandering about seeking for anything they could find to eat, even picking up grains of corn that were scattered around where the Yankees had fed their horses.[107]

Around Christmastime, General Sherman closed the noose around the garden city of Savannah and prepared to reduce it to ashes as he had done Atlanta. However, he found the Savannah people far less willing to sacrifice their city's elegance and grace on the altar of Southern independence, and he accepted their surrender without having to fire a shot (a point of contention between Atlanta and Savannah natives yet today).

He then wired an ominous telegraph message to the top general in Washington. It

Buildings in Atlanta show damage caused by Union mortar. After the city fell to the invading Yankees, General Sherman boasted that his troops had left the city "smouldering and in ruins."

read, "The whole army is burning with an insatiable desire to wreak vengeance upon South Carolina. I almost tremble at her fate, but feel that she deserves all that seems in store for her."[108]

Rocking the Cradle of Secession

General Sherman was not exaggerating his army's hatred for the state of South Carolina. They had long considered South Carolina to be the instigator of the war by leading the South in secession and commencing hostilities at Fort Sumter in Charleston Harbor. Her statesmen had proudly borne the title "fire-eaters" for their rabble-rousing oratory, and the invading Yankees intended to humble them with a little fire of their own.

The blazing violence intensified as soon as they crossed the state line. In one instance, the Federals captured and summarily executed a citizen suspected of firing on them in spite of his ardent pleas and denials. In another, the Yankees hanged several clearly innocent Southern civilians after Rebel bushwhackers in that area sniped (shot at from concealment) at them and got away. "Bummers," foragers who had cut themselves off from the army, coarsely demanded to be served sumptuous meals from Southerners before stealing everything of value and setting fire to the homes of their hosts. "They marauded through the country committing every sort of outrage," a Yankee confessed. "The country was necessarily left to take care of itself and became a 'howling waste.'"[109]

But of all the depredations loosed upon "the Cradle of Secession," none shocked the South any more than the sacking and burning of Columbia, the state capital. No one ever confirmed who started the conflagration—each side blamed the other—but General Sherman later admitted that, either way, he "never shed any tears over the event."[110] A Union officer later wrote, "The burning houses, lighting up the faces of shrieking women, terrified children and frantic, raving, drunken soldiers, formed a scene which no man of the slightest sensibility wants to witness a second time."[111]

Union "bummers" (pictured) terrorized the Southern countryside, foraging for food and stealing everything of value.

The Black Plymouth

After Sherman "liberated" South Carolina, the secretary of war, Edwin Stanton, traveled to Charleston to meet with ex-slaves and their leaders. He first asked them whether they wanted to live in integrated or segregated communities, to which the blacks unanimously replied, "Segregated." Stanton then offered them land for the taking in the Charleston area, surveyed out as a town with lots and public grounds. Thousands rushed to own their piece of America, happily submitting to the authority of the local government—local government that they themselves would conceive, support, and administer. For the first time in America, community of blacks would rule over themselves, maintaining order and solving their own problems.

A few months later, an antislavery journal jubilantly reported:

The colonists selected their lots, laid out a village, numbered their lots, put numbers in a hat, and drew them out. It was Plymouth colony repeating itself. They agreed that if any others came to join them, they should have equal privileges. So blooms the *Mayflower* on the South Atlantic coast!

However, the "colony" never grew into the thriving city that many had hoped it would. Many of the residents decided that there were greater opportunities for advancement within the mainstream of the newly integrating America. And perhaps it is best that such government-supported social experiments did fail. For had the blacks remained happily segregated on them, they might have been relegated to their "reservations" in much the same way that the Native Americans were and had their integration into American society similarly delayed.

Two days later, when the flames finally died down, two-thirds of the city lay in ruins, thousands more whites had been forced to the roads, and even more newly freed slaves choked the hordes already following Sherman's army in search of equality. Regrettably, there was another expression of equality unearthing itself throughout the South: an equality of Southerners—black, white, young, and old—sharing equitably in the hunger, hardships, and hell of the Confederacy's final death throes.

When the South began its last groaning fall, it did so in several different places: the Shenandoah Valley, the Carolinas, Petersburg, and middle Tennessee. Union general Philip Sheridan torched the last building in the Shenandoah and headed South to decimate a sizable detachment of Lee's Rebels at Five Forks, west of Petersburg. General Sherman chased the remnants of the Carolina Confederates into North Carolina and closed in on them from three indefensible sides.

The Southerners' last offensive hope, a desperate flanking maneuver northward through Tennessee, disintegrated into gory disasters at Franklin and Nashville. At the same time, the final two ports supplying the Rebels—Wilmington, North Carolina, and Mobile, Alabama—fell to the relentless Yankees. General Lee believed that his only hope for Petersburg and, hence, Richmond was to

The Federals unleashed their rage on South Carolina—the state considered to be "the Cradle of Secession"— by leveling homes and entire cities.

somehow break through the Union lines encroaching upon them. His weary men bravely attempted an all-or-nothing attack against Fort Stedman, but it failed with shocking losses, forcing him to at last order the evacuation of the capital.

A Richmond woman recalled:

I was awakened suddenly by four terrific explosions [Confederates blowing up their own supplies to prevent their capture]. Soon fire spread, shells in the burning arsenals began to explode. Flakes of fire fell around me, glass shattered and chimneys fell. Looking down from the upper end of the square, I saw a huge wall of fire blocking out the horizon. In a few hours, nothing was left except tottering walls and smouldering ruins.[112]

The gutting fires, however, only began the nightmare. An anarchy of looting and pillaging erupted during the time after the Rebels pulled out and before the Yankees arrived. The same woman described it:

The ending of the first day was truly horrible. Some Negroes of the lowest grade and miserable poor whites drank

themselves mad with liquor scooped from the gutters [large kegs of which had been dumped there by Confederates to keep them from falling into Union hands]. Reinforced by convicts escaped from the penitentiary, they tore through the streets, carrying loot from the burned district. The experience was not pleasant.[113]

Not pleasant, indeed. A Rebel straggler remembered it this way:

The streets ran with liquor. An ocean of flame was dashing as a tidal wave of destruction from street to street. Miles on miles of fire; mountain piled upon mountain of black smoke. It was one ceaseless babel of human voices, crying, shouting, cursing; one mighty pandemonium of woe.[114]

The next day Richmond lay in smoking ruins. And in an era of warfare that still equated the capture of the enemy's capital with the capture of the enemy's king in chess, the Confederate dream of independence was undeniably in check and only a few moves away from checkmate.

From Front Yard to Front Parlor

No one had watched those final moves with any more interest or apprehension than Wilmer McLean, a farmer and merchant living in Appomattox Court House, Virginia. He knew that General Lee's ragged Confederates were headed there from Petersburg and Richmond in the desperate hope of uniting with other scattered remnants in gray. He also knew that General Grant was pursuing close behind and would probably overtake Lee somewhere around his village.

Wilmer McLean's interest was more personal than most because he and his family had already endured the horrors of war during the very first battle at Manassas, Virginia. His plantation house there had been taken over and used as Confederate headquarters and later as a blood-drenched hospital. A cannonball tore through his kitchen at one point, convincing him that he should move farther south to escape the fighting.

He ended up in Appomattox Court House far removed from the rest of the war's action, but now he found himself caught up in its tragedy once again, this time as the host of the official surrender ceremony (the Confederates had commandeered his house for that purpose because it was the finest in the village).

McLean did his best to convince himself that something as peaceful as a treaty signing could not possibly cause him any property loss. And, indeed, while he and his family

Soldiers of Liberation?

Southern whites were not the only ones to feel the hot breath of Yankee wrath. Black slaves, the very people the Yankees had supposedly been sent down South to rescue, oftentimes received the harshest treatment of all. The raping of black women made its way into the Union army's own official records far more often than reports of punishment for it. Telling phrases such as "indecent outrage," "debauching females," "prey of lust," "abused by scoundrels," and "committing rapes on negroes" liberally season the Federal accounts.

Looting and robbery of blacks did not go unmentioned either. "Depredations," "stealing," "destruction of personal property," "indiscriminate pillage," and "robbing them of their money" are all well-represented entries. Other haunting refrains include "killed a little girl," "shot by a drunken soldier," "shot and killed her for resisting (being raped)," and "firing so as to cause a colored woman to lose her arm."

When investigating the matter for the secretary of war, a Union general concluded:

I found the prejudice of color and race here in full force, and the general feeling of the army of occupation was unfriendly to the blacks. It was manifested in various forms of personal insult and abuse, in depredations, stealing, and destroying their crops and domestic animals.

One indignation that Yankee soldiers regularly heaped upon blacks volunteering for battle went something like this: "We'd rather have hogs than niggers! At least, we could eat the hogs!" How long would it be before freedom had any real meaning for the blacks?

The bloodshed of the Civil War ended in the parlor of the Appomattox Court House (pictured) in Virginia when the Confederates surrendered to the Federals in April 1865.

waited upstairs, the most solemn, sacred, and meaningful ceremony of the Civil War took place in near-religious stillness beneath him. He proved to be wrong about the property loss, though. As soon as Generals Lee and Grant concluded their meeting and left, Yankee souvenir hunters stripped McLean's house of every item that was not affixed or otherwise immovable. For all of his damages, however, he was at least able to boast thereafter, "The war began in my front yard and ended in my front parlor."[115]

In a very real sense, every citizen of the South through whose fields, hills, and homes the scourge of war had passed could have made that same claim, for nearly every battle had been fought on Southern soil. Virginians and Tennesseans endured the most actual battlefield bloodshed and the depredations caused by the foraging armies who shed it. Georgia and South Carolina suffered the greatest damage intentionally directed at civilians, and in an odd, defiant sort of way they took a stubborn pride in that. It would take years, though, for most Southern civilians to decide whether any "bragging rights" they might have accrued by taking a stand in America's most significant conflict would ever fill the dull, aching chasm where their dreams for the future had once lived.

Nightmares and Corn Sprouts

And so it was over for the Southern people: a decade of dreaming of independence, two bloody years in which they almost achieved it, and two bloodier years yet watching it slip away until nothing remained of the dream but smoldering ashes, barren fields, and gloom. Some things, however, did not pass away with the defeat: shortages, hunger, homelessness, disease, grief, loneliness, and despair. For the tattered survivors of the Southern holocaust, soldiers and civilians alike, the youthful innocence with which they had plunged their hearts and their culture into "the Cause" had grayed away into prematurely enfeebled old age. And no one escaped the effects.

Wounds Enough for Everyone

One Southern citizen who suffered the Union occupation wrote, "When the war closed in 1865, the South presented a spectacle of wreck and prostration without parallel in modern times. The people had shared in the general wreck, and looked poverty-stricken, careworn, and dejected." [116] After lamenting the loss of the South's genteel lifestyle, the diarist Mary Chesnut mused, "Now we have only burned towns, deserted plantations, and sacked villages. Yes, poverty, with no future and no hope. We are exiles in our own land." [117]

Rich and poor, male and female, young and old; all shared a common misery. Wives grieved over their dead husbands. Sweethearts recoiled from maimed lovers and mothers wailed for sons who returned from the fighting armless or legless or who did not return at all. Sisters and fathers, brothers and grandparents all feared the dark brooding silences into which their battle veterans so often lapsed while women gasped awake in bed when their men screamed out from sweaty nightmares.

And the forlorn warriors just as often returned to loved ones who were suffering every bit as severely as themselves. They found anxious wives, emaciated sweethearts, and a crop of new headstones in the family burial plots. Veterans were forced to share their own haunted silences with those of their children, grim-eyed boys and girls who had forgotten how to laugh and play and remember what their fathers had been like before the war. The men tried (but usually failed) to comfort their family members' nightmares of bombardments and fires, refugees and starvation only to return to the twisted mire of their own. Throughout the South, the catastrophe remained the same for all victims of the war. The only thing that separated them was the manner in which they responded to it.

The Depressed

Ironically, it was often the former slaves who were best able to appreciate the enormity of that catastrophe. While certainly not all

A wounded Confederate soldier is nursed back to health by compassionate Northerners. Many families, both in the North and the South, were devastated by the Civil War and could not cope with the injuries or deaths of their sons, fathers, and husbands.

blacks reserved any sympathy for the white men's plight, one ex-slave suggested a measure of compassion for his one-time owner as he set off on the road to freedom.

"The master had three boys go to the war," he said,

> but there wasn't one come home. All the children he had was killed, he lost all his money, and the house soon begun dropping away to nothing. Us niggers one by one left the old place, and the last time I seed the home plantation I was standing on a hill. I looked back on it for the last time through a patch of scrub pine, and it looked so lonely. There wasn't but one person in sight, the master. He was a-setting in a wicker chair in the yard looking out over a small field of cotton and corn. There was four crosses in the graveyard on the side of the lawn where he was setting. The fourth one was his wife.[118]

Seventy-year-old Edmund Ruffin, the fire-eating secessionist who had fired one of the first shots on Fort Sumter, represented an even more extreme reaction to the Confederate defeat. Unable to live alongside what he called "the perfidious, malignant, and vile Yankee race,"[119] he wrote a final, disconsolate entry in his diary, wrapped himself in a Confederate flag, and blew his own head apart.

The Defiant

Not all Southerners reacted to the desolation with such debilitating depressions as these. Sarah Morgan proclaimed in her diary, "Submission? Never! Let a great earthquake swallow us up first! Let us leave our land and emigrate to any desert spot on the earth, rather than return to the Union!"[120] And that, in fact, is exactly what thousands of Southerners did.

After the close of the Civil War, the radical secessionist Edmund Ruffin (pictured) chose to end his life rather than live in the Union. Other defiant Southerners left the Union and immigrated to Mexico, Cuba, and Brazil.

Rebel general Jo Shelby, for example, had sworn many times that he would never lay down his arms and, true to his word, he headed for Mexico at the end of the war accompanied by three other generals, the governors of Texas and Louisiana, and about one thousand of his most dedicated cavalrymen. Fully intending to fight on as mercenaries for the pro-Confederate Mexican government, his brigade's services were declined and the unrepentant Rebels ultimately scattered as colonists throughout Mexico, Cuba, and Brazil. Others, most notably Jesse James, put their martial skills to practice in the American West as gunfighters, thieves, and desperadoes while unsung thousands immigrated to the frontier as honest cowboys, farmers, and miners.

The Free

Blacks, whose very status as human beings had suddenly been revolutionized, faced some of the most extreme and shocking adjustments to the new order. They not only had to suddenly make a living within the physical wreckage of the South, they also had to redefine their roles and possibilities as they did it. Many took to the roads going to the North, seeking but rarely finding any more acceptance up there than they had in the South. A smaller number went west and began the long task of proving themselves as frontiersmen.

The majority of ex-slaves, however, remained where they were, choosing the comfort of familiarity over the uncertainty of change. Many worked for a pittance as wage-laborers while most sharecropped for less on white-owned plantations. In any event, their lot was not a pleasant one as this ex-slave's bitter remembrance indicates:

Lincoln got the praise for freeing us, but did he do it? He give us freedom without giving us any chance to live to ourselves and we still had to depend on the Southern white man for work, food and clothing, and he held us out of necessity and want in a state of servitude but little better than slavery.[121]

The Bound and the Determined

The overwhelming majority of Southerners, however, the destitute white people who had formerly enjoyed a middle-class lifestyle, did not flee the country, move out West, shoot themselves, exploit black labor, or give up altogether in hopeless apathy. Following Robert E. Lee's final admonition to his men to "go home and make as good citizens as you have soldiers," they rolled up their sleeves and got to work rebuilding their homes, their lives, and their "country."[122]

Enterprising men recognized desperate needs and earned a living satisfying them. They fixed railroads, strung telegraph lines, cleared rivers and harbors, set up sawmills, and manufactured artificial limbs. Others bred mules and horses, melted down cannonballs into sheet iron, mined coal, and renovated shipyards. Those previously educated

Way Down South in Dixie

Southerners who refused to submit to the "foreign rule" of Union occupation forces sometimes fled the country with whatever valuables they had managed to salvage. Traveling by ship, many of them headed for Brazil, a slave-holding nation sympathetic to the Confederate cause. Once there, they formed their own community and plantations much like those they had left behind. They learned to speak the native tongue, Portuguese, but never fully forgot who they were. Their descendants live on in Brazil, and, as Jack Epstein's article in the Christian Science Monitor *reveals, they still remember the dreams that spawned them.*

"Under fluttering Confederate flags, women in hoop skirts dance the Virginia reel with men wearing Rebel gray. It could have been a gathering of Civil War buffs in Georgia or Alabama, but this picnic took place more than 4,000 miles below the Mason-Dixon line.

Brazilian descendants of confederate veterans who sought refuge in this tropical nation 130 years ago gather four times a year to celebrate their American roots. They are members of the Fraternidade Descendencia Americana, founded in 1954 to preserve ties to U.S. culture among an estimated 100,000 heirs of the original emigrants.

The Confederate emigres were some 20,000 Southerners who preferred the Brazilian wilderness to life under Yankee rule after the Civil War. The expatriates were called Confederados and their community was Vila Americana or "American Town." Today, Vila Americana (pop. 200,000) is the only city in Brazil with a coat of arms that has a Confederate flag as its centerpiece.

It would seem that some dreams never die."

Confederate soldier Jesse James (pictured) served in the army at age seventeen. After the South's surrender, he headed west, becoming a notorious gunfighter and outlaw.

took up law and medicine, architecture and the fine arts, writing books, editing newspapers, and preaching the gospel.

But of all the occupations available after the war, by far Southerners attempted farming the most often. The majority of citizens had been successful at it before the cataclysm and, despite the scorched earth, they thought that perhaps they could still coax a crop out of the ashes. And so it was in the spring of 1865 that these undaunted men and their families prayed, hoped, and planted their corn seed as if their lives depended upon the result. Then they waited. They watched. They prayed ever harder. And when the first tender sprouts popped up fresh and bright green, they rejoiced to their God that they had survived.

Notes

Introduction: The Homecoming

1. Quoted in John Richard Dennett, *The South as It Is*. New York: Viking, 1965.
2. Quoted in Shelby Foote, *The Civil War: A Narrative*. New York: Random House, 1958.
3. J. T. Trowbridge, *The South: A Tour of Its Battlefields and Ruined Cities*. Hartford, CT: Stebbins, 1866.
4. Quoted in Carl Schurz, *Reminiscences*. New York: McClure, 1907.
5. Quoted in Dennett, *The South as It Is*.
6. Quoted in Whitelaw Reid, *After the War: A Tour of the Southern States*. New York: Harper & Row, 1965.
7. Quoted in Schurz, *Reminiscences*.

Chapter 1: The Manor, the Man, and the Moment

8. Quoted in Lyle Saxon, *Old Louisiana*. New Orleans: The Century Co., 1929.
9. Mary Boykin Chesnut, *A Diary from Dixie*. Cambridge: Harvard University Press, 1949.
10. Chesnut, *A Diary from Dixie*.
11. Quoted in William C. Davis, *First Blood: Fort Sumter to Bull Run*. Alexandria, VA: Time-Life Books, 1983.
12. Sam R. Watkins, *"Co. Aytch."* New York: Macmillan, 1962.
13. Quoted in Bell Irvin Wiley, *The Life of Johnny Reb*. Baton Rouge: Louisiana State University Press, 1943.
14. Chesnut, *A Diary from Dixie*.
15. Quoted in Clement Eaton, *A History of the Southern Confederacy*. New York: Macmillan, 1954.
16. Quoted in Bruce Levine, *Half Slave and Half Free*. New York: Hill and Wang, 1992.
17. Quoted in Saxon, *Old Louisiana*.
18. Quoted in Saxon, *Old Louisiana*.
19. Quoted in Saxon, *Old Louisiana*.
20. Quoted in Richard B. Harwell, *The Confederate Reader*. New York: Longmans, Green, 1957.

Chapter 2: The Ladies Fair and Their Domain

21. Quoted in Katherine Jones, *Heroines of Dixie: Spring of High Hopes*. New York: Bobbs–Merrill, 1955.
22. Sarah Morgan, *Civil War Diary of a Southern Woman*. New York: Simon & Schuster, 1991.
23. Quoted in Page Smith, *Trial by Fire: A People's History of the Civil War*. New York: McGraw-Hill, 1982.
24. Quoted in Levine, *Half Slave and Half Free*.
25. Quoted in Levine, *Half Slave and Half Free*.
26. Quoted in Jones, *Heroines of Dixie: Spring of High Hopes*.
27. Chesnut, *A Diary from Dixie*.
28. Quoted in Saxon, *Old Louisiana*.
29. Quoted in Saxon, *Old Louisiana*.
30. Marc McCutcheon, *Everyday Life in the 1800s*. Cincinnati, OH: Writer's Digest Books, 1993.
31. Quoted in Jones, *Heroines of Dixie: Spring of High Hopes*.
32. Quoted in Jones, *Heroines of Dixie: Spring of High Hopes*.

33. Quoted in Steven A. Channing, *Confederate Ordeal: The Southern Home Front*. Alexandria, VA: Time-Life Books, 1984.

34. Quoted in Foote, *The Civil War: A Narrative*.

Chapter 3: The "Fortunate" Few

35. Quoted in Levine, *Half Slave and Half Free*.

36. Quoted in Levine, *Half Slave and Half Free*.

37. Quoted in A. Mellon, *Bull Whip Days*. New York: Weidenfeld and Nicolson, 1988.

38. Quoted in Mellon, *Bull Whip Days*.

39. Quoted in Elizabeth Fox-Genovese, *Within the Plantation Household*. Chapel Hill: University of North Carolina Press, 1988.

40. Quoted in Mellon, *Bull Whip Days*.

41. Quoted in James Blassingame, *The Slave Community*. New York: Oxford University Press, 1979.

42. Quoted in Fox-Genovese, *Within the Plantation Household*.

43. Quoted in Fox-Genovese, *Within the Plantation Household*.

44. Quoted in Fox-Genovese, *Within the Plantation Household*.

45. Quoted in Blassingame, *The Slave Community*.

46. Quoted in Elizabeth Silverthorne, *Plantation Life in Texas*. College Station: Texas A&M University Press, 1986.

47. Robert W. Fogel, *Without Consent or Contract*. New York: Norton, 1989.

48. Quoted in Mellon, *Bull Whip Days*.

49. Quoted in Mellon, *Bull Whip Days*.

50. Quoted in Julius Lester, *To Be a Slave*. New York: Scholastic, 1968.

Chapter 4: The Muscle That Made the Money

51. Quoted in Lester, *To Be a Slave*.

52. Quoted in Silverthorne, *Plantation Life in Texas*.

53. Quoted in Blassingame, *The Slave Community*.

54. Quoted in Jack Larkin, *The Reshaping of Everyday Life*. New York: HarperCollins, 1988.

55. Quoted in Larkin, *The Reshaping of Everyday Life*.

56. Quoted in Larkin, *The Reshaping of Everyday Life*.

57. Quoted in Larkin, *The Reshaping of Everyday Life*.

58. Quoted in Lester, *To Be a Slave*.

59. Quoted in Lester, *To Be a Slave*.

60. Quoted in John F. Bayliss, *Black Slave Narratives*. New York: Macmillan, 1970.

61. Quoted in Bayliss, *Black Slave Narratives*.

62. Quoted in Bayliss, *Black Slave Narratives*.

63. Quoted in Bayliss, *Black Slave Narratives*.

64. Quoted in Bayliss, *Black Slave Narratives*.

65. Quoted in Bayliss, *Black Slave Narratives*.

66. Silverthorne, *Plantation Life in Texas*.

Chapter 5: The Forgotten Majority

67. Larkin, *The Reshaping of Everyday Life*.

68. Quoted in Larkin, *The Reshaping of Everyday Life*.

69. Quoted in Juanita Leisch, *An Introduction to Civil War Civilians*. Gettysburg, PA: Thomas Publications, 1994.

70. Larkin, *The Reshaping of Everyday Life*.
71. Quoted in Wiley, *The Life of Johnny Reb*.
72. Quoted in Jones, *Heroines of Dixie: Spring of High Hopes*.
73. Quoted in Leisch, *An Introduction to Civil War Civilians*.
74. Quoted in Jones, *Heroines of Dixie: Spring of High Hopes*.
75. Quoted in Bell I. Wiley, *Plain People of the Confederacy*. Chicago: Quadrangle Books, 1963.

Chapter 6: Mountaineers, "Crackers," and Other "Traitors"

76. Quoted in Darryl Lyman, *Civil War Quotations*. Conshohocken, PA: Combined Books, 1995.
77. Edward King, *The Great South*. New York: American, 1874.
78. King, *The Great South*.
79. Quoted in Lyman, *Civil War Quotations*.
80. Quoted in Channing, *Confederate Ordeal*.
81. Quoted in Geoffrey Ward, *The Civil War: An Illustrated History*. New York: Alfred Knopf, 1990.
82. Quoted in Ward, *The Civil War*.
83. Channing, *Confederate Ordeal*.
84. Quoted in Channing, *Confederate Ordeal*.
85. Quoted in Bell I. Wiley, *Embattled Confederates: An Illustrated History of Southerners at War*. New York: Bonanza Books, 1964.
86. Quoted in Wiley, *Embattled Confederates*.
87. Quoted in Lyman, *Civil War Quotations*.
88. Quoted in Wiley, *Embattled Confederates*.
89. Quoted in Wiley, *Embattled Confederates*.
90. Quoted in Channing, *Confederate Ordeal*.
91. Quoted in Wiley, *Plain People of the Confederacy*.
92. Quoted in Ward, *The Civil War*.
93. Quoted in Channing, *Confederate Ordeal*.

Chapter 7: Total War/Utter Destruction

94. Quoted in Jerry Korn, *War on the Mississippi: Grant's Vicksburg Campaign*. Alexandria, VA: Time-Life Books, 1985.
95. Quoted in Milton Meltzer, *Voices from the Civil War*. New York: Crowell, 1989.
96. Quoted in Foote, *The Civil War: A Narrative*.
97. Quoted in Smith, *Trial by Fire*.
98. Quoted in Smith, *Trial by Fire*.
99. Quoted in Henry Steele Commager, *The Blue and the Gray*. New York: Fairfax Press, 1982.
100. Quoted in Smith, *Trial by Fire*.
101. Quoted in Ronald H. Bailey, *Battles for Atlanta: Sherman Moves East*. Alexandria, VA: Time-Life Books, 1985.
102. Quoted in Lyman, *Civil War Quotations*.
103. Quoted in Lyman, *Civil War Quotations*.
104. Quoted in Bailey, *Battles for Atlanta*.
105. Quoted in David Nevin, *Sherman's March: Atlanta to the Sea*. Alexandria, VA: Time-Life Books, 1986.
106. Quoted in Nevin, *Sherman's March*.
107. Quoted in Commager, *The Blue and the Gray*.
108. Quoted in Lyman, *Civil War Quotations*.

109. Quoted in Commager, *The Blue and the Gray.*
110. Quoted in Jerry Korn, *Pursuit to Appomattox: The Last Battles.* Alexandria, VA: Time-Life Books, 1987.
111. Quoted in Korn, *Pursuit to Appomattox.*
112. Quoted in Commager, *The Blue and the Gray.*
113. Quoted in Commager, *The Blue and the Gray.*
114. Quoted in Bruce Catton, *The American Heritage Picture History of the Civil War.* New York: Bonanza Books, 1960.
115. Quoted in Ward, *The Civil War.*

Conclusion: Nightmares and Corn Sprouts

116. Quoted in Smith, *Trial by Fire.*
117. Quoted in Smith, *Trial by Fire.*
118. Quoted in Foote, *The Civil War: A Narrative.*
119. Quoted in Ward, *The Civil War.*
120. Morgan, *The Civil War Diary of a Southern Woman.*
121. Quoted in Lester, *To Be a Slave.*
122. Quoted in Bruce Catton, *A Stillness at Appomattox.* Garden City, NY: Doubleday, 1981.

For Further Reading

Irene Hunt, *Across Five Aprils*. New York: Berkley Books, 1964. Accurate and moving historical novel of a young boy's struggle to understand why his border state family is dividing over the Civil War. Excellent glimpse of daily farm life during that period.

Katherine Jones, *Heroines of Dixie: Spring of High Hopes*. New York: Bobbs-Merrill, 1955. Collection of firsthand accounts written by Southern women at the beginning of the war. Captures the thrills, excitement, and promise of their new independence.

Katherine Jones, *Heroines of Dixie: Winter of Desperation*. New York: Bobbs-Merrill, 1955. Companion to *Spring of High Hopes*. Together, the two books hauntingly juxtapose the joy of the war's beginning with the sorrow of its end. All entries are written personally and reveal much about the day-to-day living of Southern people during the struggle.

Maury Klein, *Life in Civil War America*. Harrisburg, PA: Historical Times, 1987. Succinct yet informative booklet describing the hardships faced by civilians in both the North and the South. Written for a general readership. Contains many black-and-white illustrations.

Juanita Leisch, *An Introduction to Civil War Civilians*. Gettysburg, PA: Thomas Publications, 1994. Adds previously underreported information to the body of knowledge, including chapters on religion, immigrant societies, marriage, and infant mortality. Many sensitively captioned photographs suggesting what the subjects might have been feeling.

Julius Lester, *To Be a Slave*. New York: Scholastic, 1968. Edited firsthand accounts of slaves in slavery. Admirably balanced reports of both planter atrocities and kindnesses. Highly readable and insightfully annotated.

Marc McCutcheon, *Everyday Life in the 1800s*. Cincinnati, OH: Writer's Digest Books, 1993. Provides a wealth of extremely interesting, out-of-the-way facts about slang, transportation, homes, fashions, occupations, and much more. Can be read cover to cover as a nonfiction book or referred to when needed as an encyclopedia.

Works Consulted

Ronald H. Bailey, *Battles for Atlanta: Sherman Moves East*. Alexandria, VA: Time-Life Books, 1985. Fine overview of the campaign in which the Federals sieged, evacuated, and burned a major Southern city. Etched into the psyche of America by the movie *Gone with the Wind*.

John F. Bayliss, *Black Slave Narratives*. New York: Macmillan, 1970. A compilation of first-person slave narratives as recorded during the 1930s by Works Projects Administration writers. Considered by many to be the most important source of primary information regarding American slavery.

James Blassingame, *The Slave Community*. New York: Oxford University Press, 1979. Helpful study of not only the physical aspects of slave culture but of the psychological ones as well. Outlines the personality types of slaves and their masters and how they determined the character of any given plantation.

Bruce Catton, *The American Heritage Picture History of the Civil War*. New York: Bonanza Books, 1960. The acclaimed dean of Civil War writers reduces the war to its elements in this visually engaging book. Artistic battlefield maps (complete with tiny soldiers in action) make the events come alive, though their condensed scale can be misleading.

Steven A. Channing, *Confederate Ordeal: The Southern Home Front*. Alexandria, VA: Time-Life Books, 1984. Excellent overview of life in the South during the Civil War. Many photographs, illustrations, and maps.

Mary Boykin Chesnut, *A Diary from Dixie*. Cambridge: Harvard University Press, 1949. Simply the best look at the Southern aristocracy during the Civil War. Told with sarcasm, wit, and self-effacing frankness.

Henry Steele Commager, *The Blue and the Gray*. New York: Fairfax Press, 1982. Well-edited and annotated primary source material canvasing the entire Civil War.

William C. Davis, *First Blood: Fort Sumter to Bull Run*. Alexandria, VA: Time-Life Books, 1983. Thorough overview of the first months of the war. Excellent maps, photographs, and illustrations.

Clement Eaton, *A History of the Southern Confederacy*. New York: Macmillan, 1954. Scholarly, if somewhat dry, text on the rise and fall of the Confederate government. Offers helpful statistics and analysis of conditions on the home front.

Robert W. Fogel, *Without Consent or Contract*. New York: Norton, 1989. Scholarly work focusing on the factual and statistical evidence for the inefficiencies and wastes of slavery.

Shelby Foote, *The Civil War: A Narrative*. New York: Random House, 1958. Three-volume set conveying the historical facts of the war with the human insight of a novelist. Entertaining and readable.

Elizabeth Fox-Genovese, *Within the Plantation Household*. Chapel Hill: University of North Carolina Press, 1988. Outstanding account of white mistresses and the black servants they controlled. Many interesting stories of black women who asserted their rights and dignity and the white women who accommodated them as much as tradition allowed.

Richard B. Harwell, *The Confederate Reader*. New York: Longmans, Green, 1957. Edited collection of primary source documents and letters. Some esoteric information that casts a new and different light on certain aspects of the Southern home front.

Edward King, *The Great South*. New York: American, 1874. Surprisingly sympathetic view of the South and its common people during Reconstruction as told by a Northerner.

Jerry Korn, *Pursuit to Appomattox: The Last Battles*. Alexandria, VA: Time-Life Books, 1987. The last weeks of the war portrayed poignantly with the trauma of Southern civilians balanced by the relief of the Northerners.

Jerry Korn, *War on the Mississippi: Grant's Vicksburg Campaign*. Alexandria, VA: Time-Life Books, 1985. Excellent and highly readable overview of the first battle in which civilians were consciously made targets. Many maps, photographs, and illustrations.

Jack Larkin, *The Reshaping of Everyday Life*. New York: HarperCollins, 1988. Fascinating study of Northern and Southern daily life in the years leading up to the Civil War. A wealth of original research and findings.

Bruce Levine, *Half Slave and Half Free*. New York: Hill and Wang, 1992. Academic treatise on slavery in America. Contains many revealing quotes from slaves and their masters. Unearths much new information on attitudes and lifestyles during the slave era.

Darryl Lyman, *Civil War Quotations*. Conshohocken, PA: Combined Books, 1995. Entertaining collection of famous, infamous, and previously unknown quotes from a wide range of soldiers, politicians, and plain folk. All placed in context by the author.

A. Mellon, *Bull Whip Days*. New York: Weidenfeld and Nicolson, 1988. Slavery as told by the former slaves themselves. Provides a vivid canvas of the horrors of slavery and the inhumanity of slave owners. Very little on slaves treated less harshly.

Milton Meltzer, *Voices from the Civil War*. New York: Crowell, 1989. More primary source material taken from diaries, newspaper articles, letters, and official records of the day. Does not attempt to cover the entire war.

Sarah Morgan, *Civil War Diary of a Southern Woman*. New York: Simon & Schuster, 1991. A younger, more idealistic perception of the war and Southern home front. Unlike the more mature and realistic Mary Chesnut, Sarah Morgan remains defiantly patriotic until the end.

David Nevin, *Sherman's March: Atlanta to the Sea*. Alexandria, VA: Time-Life Books, 1986. Another excellent Time-Life Book. This one vividly exposes the reasons why Sherman came to be regarded by Georgians as "Satan himself."

Whitelaw Reid, *After the War: A Tour of the Southern States*. New York: Harper & Row, 1965. A Northern writer describes the South in the wake of the Civil War. Rich with anecdotes, sympathy, and humor.

Lyle Saxon, *Old Louisiana*. New Orleans: The Century Co., 1929. Glows with the warm ambience associated with the best of plantation living. Exposes the excesses as well.

Carl Schurz, *Reminiscences*. New York: McClure, 1907. Firsthand account of the war's conclusion as experienced by a Union officer. Shows surprising compassion for the Southern people.

Elizabeth Silverthorne, *Plantation Life in Texas*. College Station: Texas A&M University Press, 1986. Vivid pen-and-ink sketches highlight this beautifully balanced account of all aspects of slave society.

Page Smith, *Trial by Fire: A People's History of the Civil War*. New York: McGraw-Hill, 1982. Scholarly work on the social aspects of the Civil War. Delineates the impact of the war on society, lifestyle, morality, and so on.

Geoffrey Ward, *The Civil War: An Illustrated History*. New York: Alfred Knopf, 1990. Book form of Ken Burns's videotape series on the Civil War. Full of humor, pathos, and the surprises that only humanity can offer.

Sam R. Watkins, *"Co. Aytch."* New York: Macmillan, 1962. The funniest yet most moving of all diaries written by a Confederate soldier. Contains humanizing facts ignored by many historians.

Bell Irvin Wiley, *Embattled Confederates: An Illustrated History of Southerners at War*. New York: Bonanza Books, 1964. An in-depth view of the hardships imposed on the Southern civilians that ultimately led to their tragic defeat.

Bell I. Wiley, *The Life of Johnny Reb*. Baton Rouge: Louisiana State University Press, 1943. Provides the reader with the most complete sketch of the common men who made up the Confederate army, the hardships they endured personally, and the ingenious ways in which they coped with them.

Bell I. Wiley, *Plain People of the Confederacy*. Chicago: Quadrangle Books, 1963. Extremely valuable insights into the daily lives of common soldiers, citizens, and slaves.

Index

toilet paper, 29
"Twenty-Slave Law," 34

Vicksburg, Mississippi,
 siege of, 80–81
Virginia Military Institute,
 32, 85
voodoo, 37

War-Time Diary of a Georgia Girl (Andrews), 11

Watkins, Sam, 15
Webster, Thomas, 30
whites
 non-slave-holding middle-
  class, 58
 poor, 12, 71–73
 social stratification
  among, 56–57
Wigfall, Louis T., 16
Wilmington, North Carolina
 fall of, 89

women
 middle-class
  role of, 23, 63–64
 proper activities for, 26
 role of, 23, 25
 wartime responsibilities
  of, 27–28

Yankees, 9
yeoman farmers, 58
 typical home of, 59–61

Picture Credits

Cover photo: North Wind Picture Archives

Archive Photos, 27

Archive Photos/American Stock, 19

Archive Photos/Welgos, 48 (bottom)

The Bettmann Archive, 14, 37, 60, 65

Brown Brothers, 13, 28, 30, 34, 40, 51, 52, 54, 57, 66

Civil War Etchings by Edwin Forbes; published by Dover Publications, Inc., 88

Corbis-Bettmann, 22, 26, 63, 67, 72

Culver Pictures, Inc., 33, 46, 76, 78 (top), 85, 87

Library of Congress, 12, 15, 25, 74, 78, 80, 81, 82, 94

National Archives, 21 (both), 56, 58, 84, 86, 90, 95

North Wind Picture Archives, 16, 38, 49, 69, 71

Peter Newark's American Pictures, 45, 97

Peter Newark's Western Americana, 9, 35, 39

Peter Newark's Military Pictures, 11

Stock Montage, Inc., 17, 48 (top), 62

About the Author

James P. Reger's interest in the home front of the American Civil War began when he was a young boy growing up in the hills of West Virginia. He heard family lore about how his ancestors hid in the backwoods of their farm, protecting their livestock from foraging armies, and how one of them died in a Northern prison for espousing Confederate sympathies. Another was murdered at the hands of Union home guardsmen, while Mr. Reger's Union-backing great-grandmother nurtured a close friendship with "Stonewall" Jackson's sister (herself a Yankee who referred to her famous brother as a "misguided traitor").

With the stories of the Civil War still alive around him, it is little wonder that Reger took such a passionate interest in the struggle. He started exhaustively reading about the war during elementary school, formalized his study at West Virginia University, and continues to immerse himself in the subject.

He now teaches history in San Diego, California, where he lives with his wife and young son. When not teaching, writing, or enjoying his family, Reger reenacts Civil War battles, portrays living history characters in schools, and explores Civil War battlefields throughout the South.